NEW FRAMEWORK

WORKBOOK

Ben Goldstein and Mark Lloyd

Richmond PUBLISHING

www.webframework.net

5

ADVANCED

Contents

1 | Attitude

Language focus

Continuous verb forms

1 Read the sentences. Is the continuous form used because the situation is temporary (T) or changing (C)?

1 There's a bus strike at the moment so I<u>'m having</u> to get up an hour earlier each morning to walk to work. <u>T</u>

2 We're now in the middle of the course, so you should find you<u>'re understanding</u> the basic principles of philosophy a little better than when we started. ___

3 The pain <u>has been getting</u> worse as the week has gone on, so she's finally decided to see a doctor. ___

4 The latest from Hillstown Stadium is that Aston Park <u>are leading</u> the Cup holders 2–1, but there's still plenty of time for everything to change. ___

5 What time do you call this? We <u>were starting</u> to think you'd had an accident! ___

6 He<u>'d been living</u> in a hotel for nearly a month by the time he found a flat he could rent. ____

2 Rewrite the sentences using an option from the box and any other words you need.

> see   ~~are seeing~~   saw   were seeing
> have seen   have been seeing
> had seen   had been seeing

1 Asif and I have managed to get tickets for the new Harry Potter film later. Do you fancy coming?
Asif and I <u>are seeing the new Harry Potter film later</u>. Do you fancy coming?

2 Despite seeing *The Godfather* over 20 times, I still get excited when it's on TV.
Although _____ *The Godfather* over 20 times, I still get excited when it's on TV.

3 Tania was devastated to learn that her best friend had started going out with John behind her back.
Tania was devastated to find out that her best friend _____ John behind her back.

4 His face was definitely familiar, but I couldn't remember where from.
I was sure _____, but I couldn't remember where.

5 The boys were spotted by the shop assistant as they were shoplifting, and he immediately called the police.
The shop assistant _____ and immediately called the police.

6 I've spent all morning looking for a cheap flight on the internet.
All morning I _____ if I can find a cheap flight on the internet.

7 I'd arranged to meet Emi for coffee this afternoon but she's just texted me to say she can't make it.
Emi and I _____ but she's just texted me to say she can't make it.

8 Although we're not such close friends these days, Dan and I still get together from time to time for a chat and a few drinks.
Although we're not such close friends these days, I still _____ for a chat and a few drinks.

Perfect verb forms

1 Read Lou's e-mail to her friend Kris. Complete it using the phrases in the box.

> a) ours will have left home
> b) he'd just started to make some friends
> c) we'd started to notice
> d) We've had
> e) Have you booked that holiday
> f) We've been here
> g) We've been able to make a few new friends
> h) the kids have started school
> i) ~~I've just got back from the shops~~
> j) we've moved into a bigger house

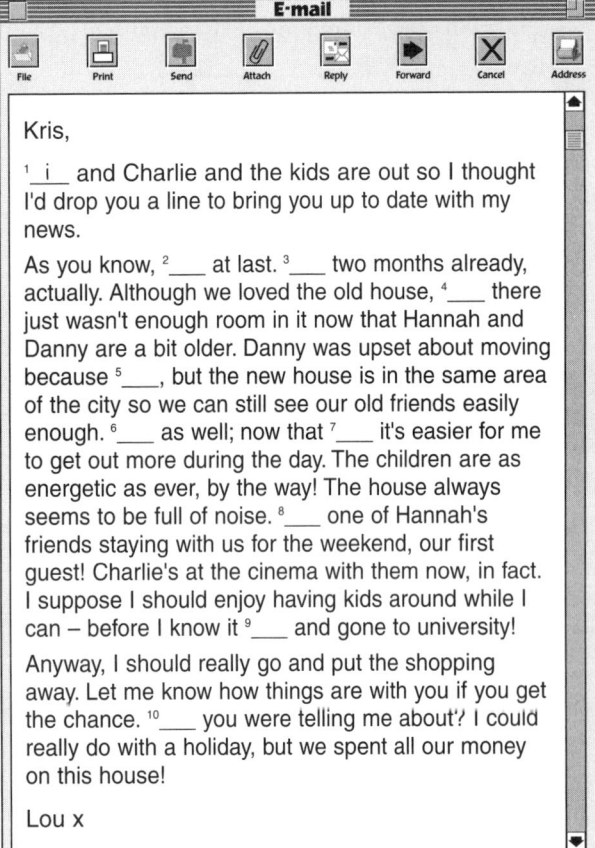

```
▣▣▣▣▣▣▣▣  E-mail  ▣▣▣▣▣▣▣▣
📄     🖨️    📧    📎    📨    ➡️    ✖️    📇
File   Print  Send  Attach Reply Forward Cancel Address

Kris,

¹_i_ and Charlie and the kids are out so I thought
I'd drop you a line to bring you up to date with my
news.

As you know, ²___ at last. ³___ two months already,
actually. Although we loved the old house, ⁴___ there
just wasn't enough room in it now that Hannah and
Danny are a bit older. Danny was upset about moving
because ⁵___, but the new house is in the same area
of the city so we can still see our old friends easily
enough. ⁶___ as well; now that ⁷___ it's easier for me
to get out more during the day. The children are as
energetic as ever, by the way! The house always
seems to be full of noise. ⁸___ one of Hannah's
friends staying with us for the weekend, our first
guest! Charlie's at the cinema with them now, in fact.
I suppose I should enjoy having kids around while I
can – before I know it ⁹___ and gone to university!

Anyway, I should really go and put the shopping
away. Let me know how things are with you if you get
the chance. ¹⁰___ you were telling me about? I could
really do with a holiday, but we spent all our money
on this house!

Lou x
```

2 Why is the perfect aspect used in each case? Is the action:

1) unfinished?   2) recent?

3) finished at an indefinite time?

Continuous & perfect verb forms

1 Choose the best option.

1 Violence in schools becomes / (is becoming) increasingly difficult to control, the Education Minister stated today.

2 As you can see from the X-ray, I'm afraid **you've broken / you've been breaking** your arm quite badly, and I think we'll have to operate.

3 I **had approached / was approaching** the junction of Queen Street and Westmore Terrace when I saw the robbery in progress,...

4 United **are creating / create** more and more chances this half, Ron. Surely they must score!

5 Quick msg 2 let u know I **passed / was passing** driving test! Party 2nite 2 celebr8! xxx

6 During the night, rain **has been moving / has moved** in gradually from the west, and it will move across the rest of the country today.

2 Were the sentences spoken or written? What was the context in each case?

Spoken stance markers

1 🔊⁽¹¹⁾ Listen to four people talking about different controversial topics. Number each topic.

Banning mobile phones in schools _____

Banning smoking at work _____

Removing speed limits on some roads _____

Allowing pubs to stay open 24 hours a day _____

2 Replace the underlined expressions with the spoken stance markers in the box.

> admittedly   all in all   apparently   basically
> frankly   inevitably   ~~presumably~~   undoubtedly

Speaker 1

1 And <u>I assume</u> everyone would go home at different times... _presumably_

2 <u>Taking everything into account,</u> I reckon it's worth a try. _____

Speaker 2

3 <u>The essential point is that</u> there are some adults who seem to enjoy spoiling kids' fun just for the sake of it... _____

4 ...and <u>the unavoidable conclusion is that</u> they're the ones trying to introduce this ban. _____

Speaker 3

5 ...<u>my honest opinion is that</u> there'll always be people who are prepared to run the risk of picking up a fine... _____

6 <u>I'm sure it's true that</u> there would be some lunatics who would let the new freedom go to their heads... _____

Speaker 4

7 <u>I've heard, though I don't know if it's true, that</u> they've already done this in parts of America... _____

8 <u>I am prepared to concede that</u> it's not good for anyone's health, so perhaps... _____

3 Now listen again and check your answers.

Vocabulary

Multiple meanings: *lift*

1 In the sentences the underlined phrase is too informal for the context. Replace them with more formal words.

1 The government has announced a plan to <u>lift</u> the law prohibiting smoking in all public places.
<u>withdraw or repeal</u>

2 You will be met at the airport and <u>given a lift</u> directly to your hotel. _____

3 A leading writer has been accused of <u>lifting her ideas from other people</u> following the publication of her latest novel. _____

4 A local man has been jailed for six months after being found guilty of <u>lifting goods</u> from a supermarket. _____

5 Police have expressed surprise that so far no witnesses have <u>lifted a finger to help</u> them with their enquires. _____

6 In cases of mild depression, regular exercise is one of the most effective ways by which sufferers may <u>give themselves a lift</u>. _____

7 If she is going to have any chance of defeating her opponent, I feel that she will have to <u>lift</u> her game considerably. _____

2 Complete the sentences with a suitable word from the list. Each word is used twice.

> fit   drag   lead   match   firm

1 Shanghai is beginning to __match__ Hong Kong in terms of its business potential.

2 Men who dress up as women and perform are sometimes known as _____ artists.

3 Anthony Hopkins played the _____ in *The Silence of the Lambs*.

4 England were no _____ for Scotland in yesterday's rugby final.

5 If you say that a person is _____, you mean that they are very attractive.

6 He's a committed environmentalist with _____ beliefs about recycling.

7 I know the pros and cons of working for a large _____.

8 I think the sofa will _____ into the van, but it's going to be tight.

9 As you're the most experienced climber, it's better if you _____ the way.

10 Some films are very slow and _____ on for ages.

Informal meanings of *attitude*

Look at the drawings. What does *attitude* mean in each case?

1 _____   2 _____   3 _____

Describing attitudes

1 Complete the gaps with adjectives which collocate with the word *attitude*.

> ambivalent   changing   favourable   hostile   new   ~~positive~~

1 It's amazing what taking a ___positive___ attitude can do! You'll feel so much better!
2 Our society has developed a whole _____ attitude to interracial issues since last year's disputes.
3 I've got this _____ attitude towards using alternative medicine; I'm not sure about it at all.
4 The survey will analyse _____ attitudes to the environment over the past century.
5 This advert helps consumers have a _____ attitude towards the product, which is essential to sales.
6 I don't know why teenagers adopt a _____ attitude to religion. They need to be better informed.

2a What do the adjectives in italics mean?

1 The government has always demonstrated an *uncompromising* attitude to drug offenders.
2 You'll have to wait a bit, they have a rather *laid-back* attitude to deadlines, you know.
3 The new boss adopted a *cavalier* attitude in his first week, sacking two members of staff in as many days.
4 The journalist had a similarly *right-on* attitude, just too trendy for my liking!

b Are the attitudes negative or positive?

Reading & Vocabulary

Complete the text using appropriate words from the box.

> creator   fasting   ~~faith~~   pilgrimage   praying   preach   prophets   worship

Although religion is often blamed for much of the conflict and unrest in the world, the major religions have a great deal more in common than many people realise. One similarity is that the followers of most religions have a deep [1] ___faith___ in the existence of a superior being or 'god'. This god is seen as the [2] _____ of all life and of the laws or 'commandments' communicated to us via human messengers, or [3] _____. Followers express devotion to their god by displaying religious objects and by [4] _____, often in special places of [5] _____, where trained 'teachers' [6] _____ to devotees and offer spiritual guidance during regular organised gatherings. Very devoted followers may show commitment to their god by [7] _____ (going without food or drink) or by making a [8] _____ to a place of particular religious significance. In terms of underlying beliefs, of course, all religions are different; however, it is worth remembering that none of them suggests that conflict and unrest are sensible ways for us to live our lives!

Listening

1 How many followers of these religions do you think there are in the UK today? Match the religions and numbers.

Buddhism	37,338,486
Christianity	144,453
Hinduism	1,546,626
Islam	329,358
Judaism	552,421
Sikhism	259,927

2 (12) Listen to three speakers. Which religion does each person belong to?

3 Listen again. Which speaker...

a) says their number is decreasing?

b) says they have no images or statues in their temples?

c) mentions a separate branch of this religion?

d) imagines that the listener knows a bit about his / her religion?

e) says worshipping together is not important?

f) explains that there are many ways of praying?

g) states that, in the UK, their religion is practised differently?

ZOOM IN: *thing*

the thing with him / her
the latest thing
just the thing
no bad thing
thing
there's no such thing
for one thing
(not) a thing
just one of those things

1 (13) Listen to the extracts (a–b) from Transcript 1.2 and complete the gaps.

a) ...*what differentiates it from groups in other countries is that there's really _____ _____ _____ as institutionalised prayer...*

b) ...*this is very different from orthodox communities – _____ _____ _____ in its attitude to women...*

2 Which expression is used:

1 for introducing one of several reasons?

2 for emphasising that something does not exist?

3 Write the correct expression from the diagram in the sentences.

1 I haven't eaten a thing all day.

2 You have to wear your hair like this; it's _____ _____ _____.

3 It's not your fault that he left you; it's _____ _____ _____ _____ _____.

4 In my opinion, _____ _____ _____ _____ as ghosts.

5 That's _____ _____ _____ _____; you never know what he's thinking.

6 I just don't like him. I mean _____ _____ _____ he doesn't wash!

7 It's _____ _____ _____ that it's raining, at least I'll get some work done.

8 A whisky is _____ _____ _____ for a cold winter night.

The Real Thing: *well*

1 (14) Listen to the extracts (1–4) from Transcript 1.2 and match with the uses (a–d).

1 *Well, I'll tell you a little about my religion.*

2 *...I'm sure you know that we worship in a mosque. Well, sometimes it's called a* masjid.

3 *Well, as I was saying, there must be just over a quarter of a million of us living in the UK at the moment...*

4 *Well, that's all for now, tomorrow we'll...*

a To return to an old topic.

b To end a discussion or a talk.

c To indicate a new topic.

d To fill a pause.

2 (15) Listen to three mini-dialogues and write down all the expressions with *well*.

3 Look at Transcript 1.5. What is the purpose of *well* in each dialogue?

4 Do you have an equivalent word for *well* in your language?

Guided writing: *A letter & e-mail to a newspaper*

1 Read this letter to a local newspaper. What problem does it describe?

A Sir,
The new occupants of the house next door frequently play loud opera music until late at night. Polite requests to reduce the volume have been met with hostility and rudeness. In the interests of finding a mutually acceptable solution, it would be helpful to know if your readers might have any suggestions.
Dorothy Plumtree
6 March

2 What was the writer's aim in writing this letter? Which of these best describes her attitude?

> angry and bad-tempered
> anxious not to cause offence
> bossy and insensitive
> sarcastic

3 What linguistic features does the writer use to indicate her attitude? Choose from the following:

> contractions   descriptive language
> ellipsis (missing out words)   factual language
> indirect questions   passive forms
> personal pronouns

4 What advice would you give to the writer? Make a list of things she could do.

5 This response was sent to the newspaper. What possible solutions are mentioned?

B Sir,
Your correspondent has two options for action over noisy and uncooperative neighbours. First, contact the local environmental health department. If this is ineffective, the second option is to take private legal action; this could be expensive, and advice should be sought. The NSCA has a neighbour-noise working group which is currently trying to establish the minimum response to noise complaints, and to recommend methods of dealing with particular problems.
Tim Brown
National Society for Clean Air
8 March

6 Read another response to letter A. What new problem is mentioned?

C Sir,
At least those with noisy neighbours have a legal remedy. What do we do about the crowds of youths who gather outside our house on Saturday evenings and spend all night riding their motorcycles up and down the road and honking their horns at each other? I do not know the identity of any of these youths, and complaints to the police have proved fruitless. We are now at the stage where we are seriously considering moving to a quieter neighbourhood.
Mary Huddlestone (by e-mail)
10 March

7 Read three responses to letter C. What solutions are suggested?

D Dear Sir,
Mary Huddlestone's distressing concerns about unruly youths are not insurmountable. May I suggest she acquires an enormous, bad-tempered dog?
A.F.
Birmingham,
12 March

E Sir,
Noisy youths on motorcycles...? An air rifle.
Yours faithfully,
Major George Witton,
by e-mail
13 March

F Sir,
Surely one effective method to discourage groups of youths from congregating outside our houses (letter, 10 March) would be to open all the windows and play loud opera music on the stereo.
Yours exasperatedly,
Rachel Williams,
Birmingham,
14 March

8 Look again at the responses (B–F) and answer the questions for each letter.
1 What is the writer's aim?
2 What is the writer's attitude?
3 What language does the writer use to express this attitude?
4 How successful is the writer in achieving his or her aim?

9 Write a letter about a local issue which concerns you. Think about:
1 your aim
2 your attitude
3 the language you can use to achieve your aim and express your attitude

10 Imagine how readers of the newspaper will react to your letter. Write an e-mail replying to your letter.

2 | Communication

Language focus

The future with *will*

1 Where would you see the following information?

① SILENCE
Exam in Progress
4.00–7.30pm

② OPENING HOURS
Mornings: 8.30–1
(Lunch: 1–3)
Afternoons: 3–6.30

③ **ROAD CLOSED FOR REPAIRS**
AUGUST 1 – SEPTEMBER 15

④ SUNAIR **Flight Details**
Name: Ms Erika Pentangeli
Depart: London Gatwick 10.05
Arrive: Malaga 13.40

⑤ LIVE IN CONCERT!
The Falling Rocks
Tonight 8pm
Tickets £25

⑥ OUTLOOK
Dry & bright at first, clouding over by late afternoon, sustained heavy rain moving in during early evening.

⑦ Kerry,
Popped out to buy a few odds & ends. Back in time for film – 8.30 OK?
Text me if not!
Phil xxx

⑧ FREE RANGE EGGS
BEST BEFORE:
14th March

a) a sign on a shop window __2__
b) a message stuck to a fridge door _____
c) a notice on the door of a classroom _____
d) a plane ticket _____
e) an extract from a weather forecast _____
f) a sign at the side of a road _____
g) a hoarding outside a concert venue _____
h) a food label _____

2 Complete the sentences using one of the verbs in the most appropriate form.

> be   ~~do~~   fly   go   have   perform
> repair   start

1 At 5pm the students _will be doing_ their exam.
2 On September 4th the workmen _____ the road for just over a month.
3 Some time during the evening it _____ to rain.
4 By 11.30 Erika _____ for nearly an hour and a half.
5 At 8.30 tonight, The Falling Rocks _____ live on stage.
6 At 2pm the shop assistants _____ lunch.
7 By the last week of March the eggs _____ off.
8 Phil _____ back by 8.30.

3 Complete the sentences with the correct form of *will*. Use words from boxes A and B as needed.

1 By 7.45pm, the students _will have finished the exam_.
2 At 6.25pm the shop assistants _____
   _____.
3 Before the end of September, the road _____
   _____.
4 At 14.00 Erika _____
   _____.
5 By 10.00, the band _____
   _____.
6 By late evening, it _____
   _____.
7 Some time after 8.30, the film _____.
8 On 13th March, the eggs _____.

Ⓐ

| preparing |
| reopened |
| raining |
| playing |
| be |
| start |
| waiting |
| ~~finished~~ |

Ⓑ

| for two hours |
| for her luggage |
| for several hours |
| to close the shop |
| ~~the exam~~ |
| OK to eat |

Cohesive devices

1 Match each situation (a–j) with one of the sentences (1–6).

a) a judge passing sentence in court ____

b) a holiday postcard ____

c) an extract from an encyclopaedia ____

d) a job reference ____

e) a medical textbook ____

f) the start of a speech ____

g) an extract from a news report ____

h) a recipe ____

i) a job application ____

j) an instruction manual for a computer ____

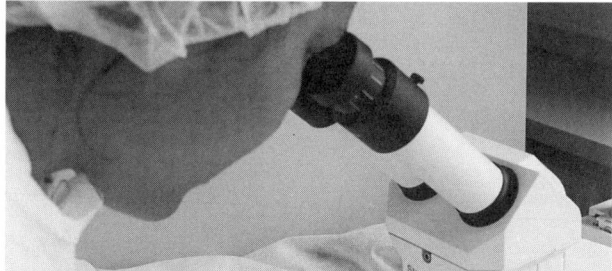
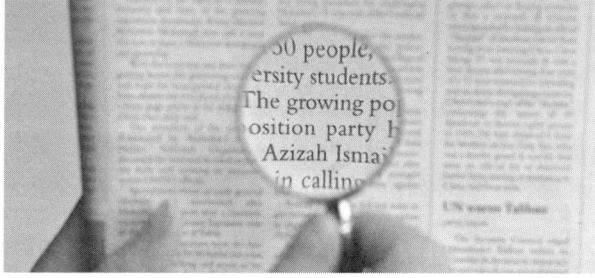

1 **To begin with / In the beginning / Firstly,** gently heat two tablespoons of olive oil in a frying pan. When the oil is hot, add the chopped onions.

2 **At the outset / At first / In the first place,** I would like to thank you all for taking the trouble to be here today despite the bad weather.

3 The Party will announce a number of new policies in its election manifesto. Its plans for education, **such as / for instance / in particular,** are said to be quite radical.

4 The nature of the crime suggests you represent a considerable danger to the public and, **accordingly / consequently / as a result of,** I have no alternative but to recommend a custodial sentence.

5 My training and qualifications are ideally suited to the post and, **as well as / furthermore / also,** I have considerable experience working in related fields.

6 The 'left-wing' parties sit to the left as seen from the president's seat, and the 'right-wing' parties sit to the right. **Hence / Thus / Otherwise** the seating indicates the political spectrum as represented in the Senate.

2 Which of the three options in bold, is *not* possible in each case?

3 Match the extracts with the four remaining situations in Exercise 1.

a) All in all, _____, I would have no hesitation in recommending Joel for any teaching position for which he were deemed to be sufficiently qualified.

b) Flight was a nightmare – lots of turbulence – and they lost one of our suitcases. _____ things improved; lovely hotel, weather hot & sunny.

c) Always eject removable disks and external players before shutting down your computer, _____ data may be lost when rebooting the machine.

d) The balloon catheter is then inserted near the blockage and inflated, _____ widening or opening the blocked vessel and restoring adequate blood flow to the heart muscle.

4 Complete each extract using one of the cohesive devices in the box.

> after that   as a result of   for instance   lastly   otherwise   such as   therefore   thus

Vocabulary

New communication words

 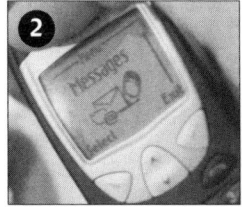 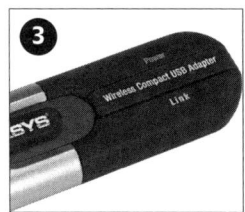  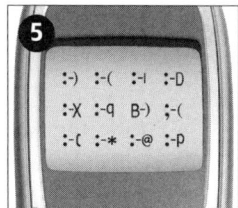

1 Match five of these new words to the images (1–5).

PDA _____   chat rooms _____   hands-free _____   spam _____

blog _____   domain _____   ring tone _____   texting _____

broadband ___4___   emoticons _____   SIM card _____   wi-fi _____

2 Are the words used in the context of mobile phones, the internet or both?

3 Complete the sentences with a word from the list.

1 Most internet connections in the world are now _broadband_.

2 It's easy to start your own website, but first you need to have _____.

3 To make your message more fun, you can add an _____ or two!

4 Young people spend so much time _____; they don't know how to write properly.

5 To keep all your numbers, all you need to do is take out your _____ and put it in this new phone.

6 A _____ supports e-mail, text messaging, web browsing and is also a mobile phone.

7 It is illegal to use a mobile phone while you're driving, so you should use a _____ car-kit.

8 You can personalize your phone by giving it a new _____.

9 When the internet first started, _____ were a popular way of getting to know people.

10 The way to be online when you're out and about is to use _____ or wireless technology.

11 Good anti-virus software will get rid of _____ as well as protecting your computer from attack.

12 You can find out what I'm doing because I'll be keeping an online journal, you know, a kind of _____.

The Real Thing: *all*

1 Look at this extract from Transcript 2.3 on page 13. Why is *after all* used?

Text messages or SMS are quick and easy to send, after all it takes a matter of seconds...

a) to say something is true

b) to give a reason

2 🎧(21) Listen to eight dialogues. Number the expressions with *all* as you hear them.

by all means ☐

for all I know ☐   by all accounts ☐

all being well ☐   **all**   all along ☐

in all ☐   for all ☐

all in all ☐

3 Listen again and match the expressions with *all* to the definitions.

according to what people say

despite

hopefully

in total

the whole time

to give permission

to say something might be true

to sum up

4 List five more expressions with *all*. Use a monolingual dictionary to help you.

Vocabulary extension

Clothes idioms

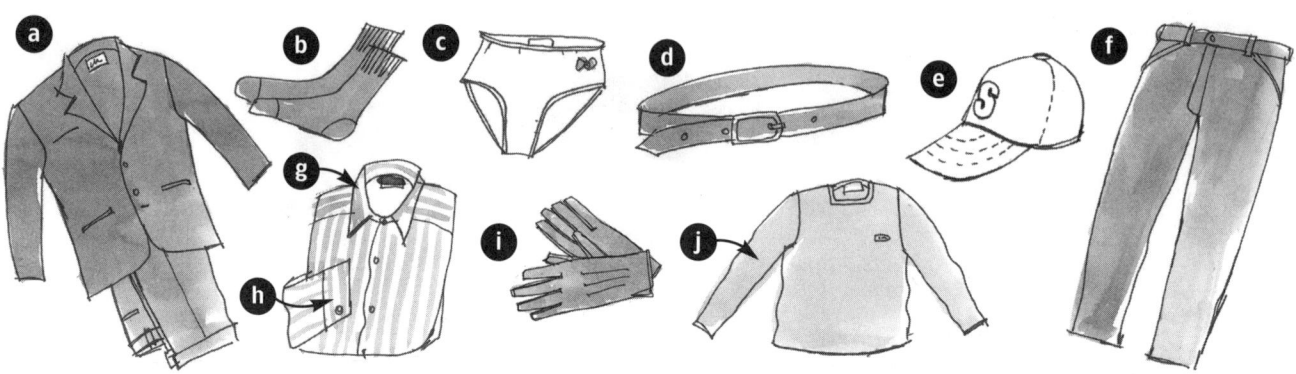

1 What clothes or parts of clothes are in the pictures?

a) _____a suit_____   f) _____

b) _____   g) _____

c) _____   h) _____

d) _____   i) _____

e) _____   j) _____

2 Complete the sentences with clothes vocabulary. Two items are repeated.

1 I'm not telling you what it is, but I have something up my _sleeve_ that I know you will like.

2 We'll have to tighten our _____ if we want to get through this month; we have so many bills to pay.

3 He got all hot under the _____ and threatened to sack me if I didn't change my attitude.

4 I always thought that she was the one who wore the _____ in that household; she always seems to get her way.

5 You'll have to pull your _____ up if you want to get an 'A' grade.

6 That was a bit below the _____. You shouldn't have made such a nasty comment.

7 They are totally inseparable, and have worked hand in _____ on this project from the start.

8 Don't get your _____ in a twist. There's nothing to get so nervous about!

9 He'd just stepped out of the shower when we arrived. There he was in his birthday _____!

10 Sometimes politicians make off-the-_____ comments and get into trouble because of it.

11 If you haven't had any ideas yet, you'd better get your thinking _____ on.

12 The police managed to _____ that guy in the end. All they needed was enough evidence to arrest him.

3 Match the expressions (1–12) with the definitions (a–l).

1 below the belt
2 to tighten your belt
3 to get your thinking cap on
4 to collar somebody (*inf*)
5 to get hot under the collar
6 to speak off-the-cuff
7 to be hand in glove with somebody
8 to get your knickers in a twist (UK *inf*)
9 to pull your socks up
10 to be in your birthday suit (*humourous*)
11 to wear the trousers
12 to have something up your sleeve

a) to get nervous or upset
b) to make a spontaneous remark
c) to try to think of a new idea
d) to be naked
e) to improve one's work
f) to be dominant / in control
g) to work very closely with somebody
h) a cruel and / or unfair comment
i) to have a secret idea
j) to arrest somebody
k) to spend less money
l) to get very angry

Takeaway English: Buying clothes: Try the interactive activity for this topic on your CD–ROM.

TAKEAWAY ENGLISH: *Creating rapport*

If you have to speak in public, creating a good relationship or *rapport* with your audience is all important.

1 **2.2** Listen to a talk about text messaging. What is wrong with the presentation?

the speaker's voice is very flat, _____,
_____

2 How could you improve it? Add two more ideas.

involve the audience more, _____,
_____

3 **2.3** Listen to another version of the same presentation. What differences can you hear?

_____, _____, _____

4 The speaker uses the following techniques to engage the audience. Listen again and write examples for each heading.

1 question tags:
2 negative question form:
3 use of *we, you, our* and *all*:
4 asides, digressions: as strange as it may seem,

Compare your answers with Transcript 2.3.

5 Rephrase these sentences using the four techniques for creating rapport from Exercise 4.

a) Mobile phone use should be banned in some public spaces.
b) People think that mobile phones are bad for your health.
c) Everyone has a mobile phone these days.
d) In some countries mobile phone use is common even in places like the cinema.

6 What is the function of these expressions? Match expressions (1–5) with uses (a–e).

1 You see, *text messaging has grown in popularity very rapidly*.
2 ...as a matter of fact, *by mid-2004 texts were being sent at a rate of...*
3 Clearly, then, *there are good reasons for its popularity*.
4 *...its use can also* actually *have serious implications*.
5 Well, *students can cheat in exams by texting answers...*

a) for example
b) this may seem surprising
c) this is important
d) this supports my last point
e) of course

How to ... use vague language

Vague language refers to language which is deliberately imprecise, non-specific or unclear. There are several reasons why we may choose to use vague language.
• Clear, accurate information may not be available or may be inappropriate.
• It may be more polite to use vague language in certain social situations.
• It can 'soften' a message and make us appear less direct or assertive.
• It can help us when we forget a word or don't have enough information.

1 Match the underlined vague language with the categories (a–d).

a) Softening a message
b) Approximating / Paraphrasing
c) Generalising
d) Replacing specific words with invented words

1 We should arrive around three-<u>ish</u>. _b_
2 <u>I don't think that was entirely fair.</u> ____

3 He's <u>the kind of</u> guy you instantly feel comfortable with. ____
4 We've had <u>all sorts of</u> trouble at work recently. ____
5 Don't you think you're <u>stretching the truth a bit</u> when you say that? ____
6 I might take a month <u>or so</u> off work and go travelling. ____
7 She's looking for a car that's small and economical. A Smart car or a Polo, <u>something along those lines</u>. ____
8 Can you pass me the <u>thingumajig</u>? It's over there on the table. ____
9 There were 20-<u>odd</u> people at the meeting. ____
10 Jon got one of those <u>whatsits</u> for his birthday, you know, those MP3 things. ____

2 Match the questions (1–10) with the responses (a–j).

1 Why has the decision been taken to reduce interest rates at this particular point in time?

2 How much does property cost round here?

3 So when do you think you'll put the house up for sale?

4 How are you feeling now? Fully recovered?

5 I've just heard about Suzie and Howard. Amazing, isn't it?

6 I've just seen that bloke who used to live next door to your sister, you know, the one who got married last year. Do you know who I mean?

7 How many people were at the match, do you think?

8 Living standards in this country have definitely improved in the last ten years, wouldn't you agree?

9 What about Lou's suggestion? Maybe it's worth a try?

10 We're running at bit late. What time do you make it?

a) Not just yet. Before we put it on the market we want to smarten it up a bit – paint the walls, shampoo the carpets, _____.

b) I'd say you're looking at £120,000 for a one-bedroom flat, _____ a few thousand.

c) Yeah, _____. My appetite isn't quite back to normal yet, but I'm a lot better than I was.

d) Actually, _____. Salaries have gone up, yes. But prices have also increased considerably, so nothing much has changed really.

e) Well, with unemployment _____ 2 million, the government wants to stimulate the economy by encouraging an increase in borrowing.

f) I know. Apparently she found out he'd been having an affair so she just told him to get lost, _____.

g) No, I think it's a terrible idea. I can think of _____ reasons why it wouldn't work.

h) It's _____ ten past four. We should be OK, as long as there are no hold-ups with traffic.

i) Oh, Gary _____? Johnson, is it? Did you speak to him?

j) Well, the stadium has a capacity of 75,000, and I'd say it was just over half full, so I reckon the attendance was 40,000, _____.

3 Complete each response using the vague language in the box.

> give or take   I'm not sure that's strictly true
> just gone   more or less
> or words to that effect   roughly speaking
> somewhere in the region of
> that kind of thing   umpteen
> whatsisname

4 (2.4) Listen and check.

5 Match the expressions to the categories (a–d) from Exercise 1.

a) Softening a message

b) Approximating / Paraphrasing

c) Generalising

d) Replacing specific words with invented words

6 Answer each question, using vague language expressions from sections 1 and 3.

1 What would your ideal house be like?

2 What is the population of the town where you live?

3 What time do you get up at the weekend?

4 How would you describe your best friend?

5 What would you say to someone who phoned you at random and tried to sell you life insurance?

3 Hate

Language focus

Adding emphasis

1 List four things that can go wrong on holiday.

1 _____   3 _____
2 _____   4 _____

2 Read the conversation and compare your ideas.

ROSA: Hi Trish, how was your holiday?

TRISH: Oh, don't ask!

R: Oh no! Why? What happened? Didn't you go in the end?

T: No, ¹ <u>we went</u>, but honestly, Rosa, everything went wrong. First the taxi to the airport broke down, so we thought we'd missed the flight. Then, when we got there, we found out the flight was delayed by five hours.

R: That was lucky!

T: Well, yes, I suppose it was, but ² <u>it also meant</u> that we had to spend the first day of our holiday sitting in a departure lounge ... and you know how Felix hates flying! So he was getting more and more nervous...

R: I bet he was!

T: Anyway, the flight itself was about the worst I've ever been on. ³ <u>Dreadful</u>. Lots of turbulence so we had to keep our seatbelts on all the time. And the food was even worse than usual; can you imagine?

R: Yeah ⁴ <u>but you've flown often enough</u> to know what airline food is like.

T: I know, but ⁵ <u>this was supposed to be</u> one of the best airlines. What a joke! The kids were off colour for the next few days, and I'm sure it was what they'd eaten on the plane.

R: How did Felix get on in the end?

T: Oh he was fine! ⁶ <u>Once he's sitting down</u> on the plane he's OK. He fell asleep before we took off and slept pretty much all the way!

R: At least something went right, then?

T: Yes, but then we got to the hotel and found it was next to a building site. In fact ⁷ <u>the hotel was a building site!</u> ⁸ <u>It wasn't like</u> the picture in the brochure. The swimming pool was only half built, the balcony we'd been promised wasn't safe, the lift was out of order nearly the whole time. ⁹ <u>The only time it worked</u> it got stuck halfway up and we had to wait for a mechanic to come and get us out! Unbelievable!

R: What about the resort? What was that like?

T: It was better than the hotel, but not by much! ¹⁰ <u>The beach was filthy</u>, covered with cigarette ends and empty beer cans, and the sea wasn't safe to go in most days. ¹¹ <u>Wandering around the shops or sitting in bars watching English football on the TV was all we did all week.</u> Felix and the kids didn't mind that too much, but it's not really my cup of tea.

R: Well, no!

T: Let's just say I ended up writing three times more postcards than usual. ¹² <u>I wrote 15!</u> I sent you two, by the way. Have you got them yet?

R: No, but they take ages to...

3 Look at the underlined parts of the conversation (1–12). How can the speaker add emphasis in each case?

4 (31) Listen and write down the words or expressions the speaker uses to add emphasis.

1 _____   5 _____   9 _____
2 we did go (c)   6 _____   10 _____
3 _____   7 _____   11 _____
4 _____   8 _____   12 _____

5 How has emphasis been added in each case? Classify your answers on page 15.

   a) Intensifiers: It's can be extremely hot in July.

   b) Sentence adjuncts: He actually missed the first train.

   c) The auxiliary *do*: I do think the UK is a good holiday destination.

   d) Prefacing phrases: The fact is...

   e) Fronting: For years I went on holiday with my parents.

   f) Cleft sentences: The thing I hate most is carrying a heavy suitcase.

6 Each sentence has a word in the wrong position. Find the word and mark where it should go.

1 She so is easy to talk to. Some doctors can make you feel uncomfortable somehow, but not her.

2 I know how unfair life can seem sometimes at your age, do believe me! I was young once, you know!

3 It looks extremely complicated, but in fact it's quite straightforward. You double-click simply on the icon and drag it across to the folder, and it should install automatically.

4 I know it sounds unlikely, but I couldn't start the car for ages and when did I finally get it going I found it had a puncture. Anyway, sorry I'm late!

5 So let me get this straight. He threatened actually to call the police because you'd parked in front of his house?

6 It totally was unreal. The guy just grabbed my phone and, like, ran off down the street.

Uses of *get*

1 Choose the correct response (a–f) to continue each conversation.

Speaker A	Speaker B
1 What did your dad say when he saw your report?	a) Yeah, I got my hair done this morning.
2 Am I imagining it or do you look different today?	b) Shall I see if I can get it going with my jump leads?
3 The car won't start. I think the battery's flat.	c) Oh, he got really mad, just as I knew he would.
4 This computer keeps crashing.	d) Oh, right. I'll get Terry to have a look at it.
5 What was the concert like last night?	e) I heard. It got hit by a car, didn't it?
6 Leanne's a bit upset this morning. Her cat died yesterday.	f) Fantastic, she even got to go backstage to meet the band!

2 Match the use of *get* in each response with one of the patterns (a–f).

   a) *get* + adjective __c__

   b) *get* (+ object) + *-ing* _____

   c) *get* + to + infinitive _____

   d) *get* + past participle _____

   e) *get* + object + past participle _____

   f) *get* + person / organisation + to + infinitive _____

3 Complete the quotations using the words or phrases in the box.

> her   made   older   ~~people~~   someone   stabbed   to drink   themselves   ~~thinking~~   to know

1 I like any reaction I can get with my music. Just anything to get __people__ __thinking__. (*Jim Morrison, American singer*)

2 Sometimes you have to get _____ _____ really well to realise you're really strangers. (*Mary Tyler Moore, American actress*)

3 Anyone who is capable of getting _____ _____ president should on no account be allowed to do the job. (*Douglas Adams, British author*)

4 Strategy is buying a bottle of fine wine when you take a lady out for dinner. Tactics is getting _____ _____ it. (*Frank Muir, British writer*)

5 I used to dread getting _____ because I thought I would not be able to do all the things I wanted to do, but now that I am older I find that I don't want to do them. (*Nancy Astor, British politician*)

6 Opera is when a guy gets _____ in the back and, instead of bleeding, he sings. (*Ed Gardner, American comedian*)

4 Match each quotation with one of the patterns in Exercise 2.

Vocabulary

Expressing annoyance

1 Look at the italicised words. Are they formal, informal or neutral?

1 You know this whole situation is *exasperating*.
   __formal__

2 What a *pain*! He's always late! _____

3 Smoking in restaurants really *bothers* me.
   _____

4 It really *gets me* that we never have enough money! _____

5 This is so *infuriating*, how many times do I need to tell you? _____

6 That really *ticks me off*, so don't do it again!
   _____

2 Rewrite each sentence in a different register using the expressions.

Informal: to bug / to piss off
Formal: bothersome (*adj*)
Neutral: to irritate / to annoy / irritating / annoying

1 __This whole situation is really bugging me.__
2 _____
3 _____
4 _____
5 _____
6 _____

3 Look at the pictures. Which idioms are illustrated?

1 It drives me up the wall. _____
2 _____
3 _____

4 _____
5 _____
6 _____

4 Which words can add emphasis to the expressions?

1 It drives me _____ up the wall. absolutely,...

2 It _____ gets on my nerves.

Vocabulary extension

bother

1 (3.2) Listen to the extracts and complete the gaps.

1 Oh, _____ _____ _____
   _____ but would you mind closing the window?

2 A: Listen, I'll give you a hand with that, it's heavy.
   B: Oh, no, please _____ _____; I can manage fine, thanks.

3 A: So, what are you up to tonight?
   B: Well, there's a party, but I'm so tired, I _____ _____ _____ to go.

4 _____ _____ _____ whether we go on holiday or not! We'll have a good time whatever we do!

5 I didn't want _____ _____ of going to the shops, so I bought it on the internet.

6 If he _____ _____ you, you should call the police.

2 What does *bother* mean in each case? Match the meanings (a–f) with the examples (1–6).

a) the inconvenience _____
b) to disturb _____
c) to worry _____
d) to harass _____
e) it's not important _____
f) it's too much effort _____

3 (3.3) Listen to the examples. Is *bother* followed by the infinitive or gerund? Which prepositions are used with *bother*?

1 __infinitive / to__   3 _____ / _____
2 _____ / _____   4 _____ / _____

4 (3.4) What does *don't bother* mean in each of the two dialogues?

1 _____
2 _____

Word-building

1 Make nouns by combining the words and suffixes.

appear	-ity	1 _____
concentrate	-ance	2 _____
enjoy	-tion	3 _____
fellow	-ment	4 _____
pure	-ship	5 _____

2 Make adjectives by combining the words and suffixes.

beauty	-able	1 _____
friend	-al	2 _____
like	-ful	3 _____
nature	-ive	4 _____
respond	-ly	5 _____
scandal	-ous	6 _____

3 Complete the table with personal qualities and characteristics.

Noun	Adjective
ambition	ambitious
_____	anxious
commitment	_____
consideration	_____
_____	generous
_____	loyal
passion	_____
respect	_____
_____	sensitive
willingness	_____

Reading

Use the correct form of the words to complete the gaps in the text.

1 perceive	6 appear
2 individual	7 sincere
3 intimate	8 mystery
4 leader	9 benefit
5 bore	10 spontaneous

Don't want to be hated?
Here are 8 tips on how to be loved!

Believe in yourself. If you do, others will. Don't wait for someone else to proclaim your talent or worth. People's [1] _perceptions_ are often formed by the signs you send out.

Reveal your inner spirit. [2] _____ is the key to becoming a star. Dare to be different and it will pay off!

Charm everyone. To charm is to seduce, this will put others at ease, create a feeling of [3] _____ and bring warmth into an otherwise ordinary situation.

Radiate charisma. This is all about believing that you have innate magnetism and powerful [4] _____ qualities.

Keep changing. Looking the same can lead to [5] _____. Altering your [6] _____ can help you gain more confidence. Be a chameleon and you will attract many different kinds of people.

Keep something back. [7] _____ is everything, but you should not reveal all. The key is not giving it all away too soon – it's better to remain just a little bit [8] _____.

Enjoy yourself. There's nothing more [9] _____ than letting yourself go. If you show that you're having a good time, others around you will too.

Be ready for the moment. [10] _____ is the greatest of gifts. When an opportunity arises, you should seize it. This will make you an exciting and inspirational person to be seen with.

Listening

 **a** ☐

 **b** ☐

 **c** ☐

 **d** ☐

 **e** ☐

 **f** ☐

1 (3.5) Listen to five people describing love / hate relationships. Match each speaker to an illustration. There is an extra option.

2 Listen again. Which speaker...

1 feels ashamed? _____

2 has professional problems? _____

3 feels optimistic at the moment? _____

4 feels a sense of estrangement? _____

5 knows when he/she is going to feel bad? _____

3 Which speakers feel that their situation is shared by others? Who feels that their situation is unusual?

ZOOM IN: *place*

1 (3.6) Listen to these extracts from Transcript 3.5 and complete the gaps to make expressions with *place*.

1 ...but when they lose, well I'm just _____ _____ the place.

2 ...she starts off saying something like, 'I know _____ _____ _____ place to criticise...'

3 He gets all the attention and I feel a bit _____ _____ place.

4 It's crazy but I guess I _____ _____ place.

5 ...you tend to feel like this is _____ place _____ me.

2 What does the *place* expression mean in each case? Which three expressions have a similar meaning?

1 To be all over the place = to be upset. _____

2 _____

3 _____

4 _____

5 _____

3 Look at the diagram. Complete the gaps with the expressions from the diagram.

to fall into place   to lose your place

neither the time nor the place — (place) — as if you own the place

going places

1 The advert said it was a car for people who are really _____.

2 I couldn't work it out at first, but then it kind of all _____.

3 I don't know if I _____ in the queue, or that guy pushed in!

4 OK, you're right but this is _____ to discuss such a serious matter.

5 Let me remind you that you're a guest in this house; I don't want to have you strutting around here _____.

4 List adjectives and nouns which collocate with *place*. Use a monolingual dictionary to help you.

Guided writing: *A Weblog*

1a Answer the questions about *blogs*.

   a) What is a blog?

   b) What does a blog look like?

   c) What topics do blogs focus on?

   d) Where did blogs come from?

   e) How can you create your own blog?

b What do these words mean?

> URL   commentary   posting   profile

2 (3.7) Listen and check your answers.

1 Free blog sites, like blogger.com, provide everything you need to get started, although a free blog may be vulnerable to spam or pop-ups. Alternatively sites such as typepad.com offer more features for a small fee. You can post photos, or add to your blog by sending text messages. Some sites offer the option of a password so you decide who reads what you've written.

2 Decide how you want your blog to look, then choose a colour scheme and layout. After designing your blog, write a few posts to test it and adjust the layout if necessary. To make your blog look more attractive, have a look at sites, like BlogSkins.com, which offer 'skins': colourful and appealing background designs for your blog.

3 Determine your purpose, main subject and your audience to allow you to adopt an appropriate tone. Blogs are for strong opinions and the more passionate you are, the more interesting your writing will be. Be sincere but accept full responsibility for your blog. There have been cases where employees have criticised their boss in a blog and been sacked as a result!

4 Link to other blogs and websites, and acknowledge your sources; your readers may enjoy the sites you visit. The internet is democratic and bloggers amplify each others' voices when they link to each other.

5 Publicise your blog in one of three ways: send the address (URL) to your friends; publish the URL on your website, if you have one; or add the URL to postings you make on other blogs. Remember to update frequently, too. Interested readers will return to your site looking for something new so try to post several times a week.

6 Be patient! Most blog audiences are small, but over time and with regular updates your audience will grow. Most importantly, remember that your blog is a gift to yourself. Blogs are the modern way for people to have fun and express themselves, and we're all invited to the party!

3 Read the six-step plan and answer the questions.

  1 What are the potential advantages of paying for a weblog?

  2 What different factors should you think about when designing your weblog?

  3 Why is it advisable to bear in mind who might read your blog?

  4 In what way is the internet 'democratic'?

  5 What advice is offered for both getting and keeping an audience?

4 You are going to start your own blog. Make notes for each stage of the six-step plan.

5 On a separate sheet of paper, plan how your blog will look. Write your first posting.

6 Read the blogs written by other students. Post your response to a blog of your choice.

4 Relationships

Language focus

Modal verbs of obligation, necessity & prohibition

1 Match the road signs with their meanings.

a) Stop here __4__
b) Low bridge ahead _____
c) 30-minute parking zone _____
d) Beware of animals in road _____
e) Slow down _____
f) Maximum speed 40 _____
g) One way _____
h) Residents' parking only _____

2 Complete the explanations for each sign using the modal verbs in the box.

> can / ~~can't~~   have to / don't have to
> mustn't   need   should / shouldn't

1 Vehicles which are more than 3 metres high __can't__ fit under the bridge which crosses the road ahead.
2 This is the top speed you are allowed to drive at, but you don't _____ to drive at this speed all the time.
3 You _____ turn left here, because traffic isn't allowed to go in that direction.
4 You _____ stop here and wait to make sure the road ahead is clear before you continue.
5 You _____ be particularly careful because there may be animals in the road.
6 You _____ only leave your car here if you live in this area.
7 You _____ keep driving so fast here because you might have to stop soon.
8 You _____ stop here, but if you want to you can leave your car here for half an hour.

Modal verbs of deduction & possibility

1 Read the dictionary definition of Sudoku and answer the questions.

> **Sudoku:** a logic-based number puzzle. Although it has a Japanese name (meaning *single number*), Sudoku was invented by a New Yorker in 1979. The aim of the puzzle is to enter a number from 1 to 9 in each square of a 9x9 grid made up of nine 3x3 boxes. Each row, column, and box must contain only one example of each number. Some numbers are already included. No mathematical ability is necessary; completing the puzzle requires only patience and logic.

1 Where and when was Sudoku invented?
_____
2 How many rows and columns make up a Sudoku grid? _____
3 How many times does each number appear in a completed Sudoku puzzle? _____
4 How important is it to be good at Maths in order to solve a Sudoku puzzle? _____

	1	2	3	4	5	6	7	8	9
A	6	8			3	7		9	1
B		1				8		2	
C	7						5	8	
D		3		1			7		5
E		6		9	4	5		3	
F	8		2			3		1	
G		4	6						8
H		7		5				4	
I	5	9		8	2			7	6

2 Read the conversation between two friends. Complete the gaps using the modal verbs in the box.

> can   can't   could   must

SALMAN: So, where do we start?

ABDUL: Well, look for the row or column with most numbers already filled in, this one here, column 8. There are two numbers missing; 5 and 6 see?

S: OK, but how do we know which goes where?

A: Easy. We know that D9 is a 5. Now, because each number appears only once in a row, the 5 here tells us that D8 a) __can't__ be a 5.

S: Aha! So it b) _____ be the 6?

A: Exactly! And the 5 c) _____ go in G8. There, our first complete column!

S: Oh, I see. It's easier than it looks, then. Let me do the next one on my own. This one here, E7. Right, this box already has a 1, 3, 5, 7 and now a 6, and row E has a 9 and a 4 as well, so E7 d) _____ be an 8, right?

A: Ah, but what about a 2? We don't have one of those yet.

S: Oh. No, we don't. So E7 e) _____ be an 8 or a 2?

A: Well, no. Look carefully. Look at the last column, there's an 8 in it, right?

S: OK. So?

A: So, neither E9 nor F9 f) _____ be an 8.

S: Oh, I see what you mean. But there's no 8 in this column, column 7. So, E7 or F7 g) _____ both be an 8. That doesn't really help us.

A: Wrong again! Look at this row here, row F, what's the first number in the row?

S: 8.

A: So?

S: So … ah, so F7 h) _____ be an 8. I see! And E7 i) _____ be an 8. Am I right?

3 Can you work out what number goes in E9? _____

4 🔊 Listen and check your answers to Exercises 2 and 3.

5 Listen again. Write the correct numbers in the Sudoku grid.

6 Choose the correct option in each case.

1 F7 **might** / **can't** be a 1 because there is already a 1 in row F. In fact, it **must** / **might** be either a 4 or a 9, because these are now the only numbers missing from this box.

2 Neither row F, column 7 or column 9 has a 4 or a 9 in it, so that doesn't help us. F7 **could** / **must** be a 4, but F9 **must** / **might** also be a 4. We'll have to come back to F7 later.

3 A7 **must** / **can't** be a 3 because there is already a 3 in row A, so a 3 **must** / **can't** go in either B7, B9 or C9 because this box doesn't have a 3 yet.

4 F5 **must** / **can't** be a 2 because a 2 already appears in F3, but it **can't** / **might** be a 6, because there isn't a 6 in row F yet.

5 The numbers in row I tell me that I6 might be a 1. It **may** / **can't** be a 3, though, because a 3 appears in column 6 already. So, both I3 and I7 **might** / **can't** be a 3.

7 Now try to complete the rest of the puzzle by making similar deductions.

Modal verbs of ability

Choose the option which is *not* possible in each case.

1 Because of reduced profits the company **can't** / **isn't able to** / **doesn't manage to** give its staff a bonus this year.

2 Do you think you **can** / **can manage to** / **can be able to** do it on your own or shall I give you a hand?

3 My cousin was one of those 'child geniuses'. By the time she was three she **was able to** / **managed to** / **could** read and write like an eight-year-old!

4 I'm afraid they'd sold out of semi-skimmed milk, but at least I **was able to** / **managed to** / **could** get some full-fat instead. I hope that's OK.

5 After failing it five times, David finally **managed to pass** / **succeeded in passing** / **could pass** his driving test.

6 It'll be really busy, so I hope we **could** / **will manage to** / **will be able to** find somewhere to park.

Vocabulary

Phrasal verbs: Relationships

1 Order the drawings (a–h) to tell the story of a conventional relationship.

2 Read the text and replace the underlined words or expressions with phrasal verbs in the appropriate tense. Make any other necessary changes.

> ask sb out   break up (with sb)   ~~chat sb up~~   fall for sb   fall out (with sb / over sth)
> get on (well) with sb   go out (together)   move in / settle down (together)   put up with sb / sth

Karl and Sophie met at a mutual friend's party. Sophie liked the look of Karl from the start. She thought she had nothing to lose and decided to ¹start talking to him, hoping to attract him. They made some small talk, discussing this and that: music, the weather, friends; nothing special. It was uncanny how ²much they liked each other, there was something weird about the way they seemed to have the same opinion about everything! Nothing more happened that night and both went home to their flats. The next day, after some careful thought on the matter, Karl ³phoned Sophie and invited her to the cinema. They went to see the latest Woody Allen film, which turned out to be the same as all the others, but they had a good time anyway. The more they talked, the more they realised how much they liked each other, they ⁴had both fallen in love – just like that!

So, they soon started to ⁵become an official couple, they became 'an item': Karl and Sophie. They went on holidays together, they met each other's families and spent all their time hanging out with each other, though they still kept their living space separate. But, it wasn't long before they decided to ⁶lead a more stable life. In the end, Karl moved into Sophie's flat and the two of them prepared to share a life together. But all it took was six months for 'cosy domesticity' to become 'a living hell'. She couldn't ⁷tolerate his moods, always up and down, and he began looking at other girls. Eventually, they ⁸had a big argument about commitment, and it became obvious that the relationship wasn't going to survive much longer. After a couple of months of trying to sort things out, they both accepted that the best thing would be for them ⁹to go their separate ways.

1 _chat him up_____
2 _____
3 _____

4 _____
5 _____
6 _____

7 _____
8 _____
9 _____

Food phrasal verbs: Try the interactive activity for this topic on your CD–ROM. **23**

Vocabulary extension

Relationship idioms

> be hung up on sb / sth
> ~~be into sb / sth~~   dump sb
> have a crush on sb
> have a soft spot for sb / sth
> have it in for sb   hit it off with sb
> think the world of sb / sth
> two-time sb   walk out on sb

1 Divide the idioms into positive and negative. Use a monolingual dictionary to help you.

POSITIVE   NEGATIVE

___be into sb / sth___   _____

_____   _____

_____   _____

_____   _____

_____   _____

2 Complete the gaps with the correct idiom.

Positive

1 I wouldn't say that I'm attracted to her, but I
__have a soft spot__ for her. I care about her, you
know.

2 As soon as we met, we just _____
immediately. It was as if we'd known each other
all our lives.

3 When you're a kid, it's normal to
_____ on your teacher at school, but
that's not really love.

4 It's a very calm relationship. I like her, she likes
me, we _____ into each other, that's
all!

5 I don't just love her, I really admire her; I mean
I just _____ of her!

Negative

6 I couldn't believe there was another man in her
life, that she had been _____ me all
along.

7 Attraction can become obsession very easily.
I'm so _____ on him now, I feel kind
of out of control.

8 I knew it wasn't going to last, but I never
thought she'd _____ me just like
that!

9 After that argument, she really
_____ for me now. I mean, she
criticises me whenever she can.

10 It's amazing, one day she just left; she
_____ on her husband and three
kids, all because of another man!

Easily-confused words

1 Look at the words in the box. Why are the words in
each pair easily confused?

> commitment / compromise   couple / partner
> date / appointment   discuss / argue
> intend / pretend   present / actual
> remind / remember   sympathetic / kind

2 Choose the correct alternative in each sentence.

1 Can I come to the party with my couple /(partner)?

2 I can't believe you've got a date / an
appointment with him. I thought you didn't like
him!

3 I'm kind / sympathetic to your feelings, but
there's not much I can do about it.

4 We spent the whole afternoon arguing /
discussing about where to go on holiday.

5 I don't know about his present / actual
girlfriend, but I never got on with the others.

6 You will remind / remember to phone me when
you get in, won't you?

7 In all relationships, you have to make some kind
of compromise / commitment.

8 I didn't pretend / intend to hurt your feelings.

3 Write definitions for the words not used in Exercise 2.

a) _couple = two people, often married_____

b) _____

c) _____

d) _____

e) _____

f) _____

g) _____

h) _____

🌐 **The same argument:** *Try the interactive activity for this topic on your CD-ROM.*

I didn't know you couldn't smoke here

1 (4.2) Listen to three dialogues. What is the situation? What is the excuse?

	1	2	3
Situation			
Excuse			

2 Listen again. Which expressions do the speakers use to introduce their excuses?

The thing is..., _____, _____

3 Look at dialogue 1 in Transcript 4.2. Find expressions which mean 'I didn't intend to'.

I wasn't aware..., _____, _____

4 How do the speakers make their apologies more emphatic?

5 Invent apologies or excuses. Try to use the expressions from Exercises 2–4.

1 A passenger asks you to stub out your cigarette in a non-smoking compartment on the train.
Terribly sorry ... I didn't realise...
I haven't got my glasses on...

2 It's your mother's 60th birthday and you haven't brought her a present.
_____

3 You arrive nearly an hour late for an important meeting with your boss.
_____

4 Your partner discovers that you've been sending romantic text messages to another man / woman. _____
_____

5 You forgot to go food shopping and there's nothing at home for the family to eat.
_____

How to ... learn phrasal verbs

Learners of English list multi-word verbs, often referred to as phrasal verbs, as an aspect of language they find difficult. There are several reasons for this:
1 There are many phrasal verbs in English.
2 Some phrasal verbs have more than one meaning.
3 The meaning of a phrasal verb is often idiomatic.

To learn phrasal verbs, it is essential to organise them into groups. There are three ways to do this:

A Organising phrasal verbs by *verb*

Organising phrasal verbs according to the main verb can be helpful.

1 The sentences include phrasal verbs with *put*. Match each one with a situation.

a) a receptionist answering the phone
b) an estate agent trying to sell a house
c) someone complaining to a neighbour
d) minutes of a local residents' meeting
e) an advertisement

1 Look, I can't put _____ this any longer. If you can't keep your children under control, I'll call the police.
2 Don't let the condition of the external paintwork put you _____. The interior is beautifully decorated.

What is the best way to learn phrasal verbs?

3 Try the new Krispichoc Low-cal Bar! Enjoy the creamy taste of milk chocolate without putting _____ weight!
4 Just one moment please. I'll see if I can put you _____.
5 Mrs Akram put _____ the idea of introducing free parking for local residents.

2 Now complete each sentence using a particle from the box.

forward   off   on   through   up with

3 List four more phrasal verbs for each verb.

1 get _up_ / _____ / _____ / _____
2 look _after_ / _____ / _____ / _____
3 pick _____ / _____ / _____ / _____
4 take _____ / _____ / _____ / _____

B Organising phrasal verbs by *particle*

Organising verbs according to the meaning of the particle can help you remember them.

1 Match each group of sentences with the general meaning of the particle *on*.

a) starting a machine or process
b) continuing an action or process
c) receiving help or support

Group 1
1 The Prime Minister is _____ on his colleagues to support him in today's vote in Parliament.
2 Don't worry; you can always __count__ on me for support.
3 In the future many countries will have to _____ on nuclear power for their electricity supply.

Group 2
4 _____ the kettle on, love. I fancy a cup of tea.
5 Make sure the cables are connected correctly before _____ on your computer.
6 Please do not _turn_ your mobile phone on until you are well inside the airport terminal building.

Group 3
7 If any letters arrive for you we'll make sure they get __sent__ on to your new address.
8 The meeting was scheduled to finish at three, but as usual it _____ on until 3.45.
9 It was such a great party we _____ on until the end.

2 Complete the sentences using a verb from the box.

> dragged   depending   put   stayed
> switching   rely

3 Match these particles with a general meaning.

Particle	Meaning
down	enter / arrive
in	leave
off	move to a higher
out	position
up	move to a lower position
	remove

4 Complete the examples with a particle from Exercise 3.

1 I'm going to dig _____ some carrots in the garden.
2 A dangerous prisoner broke _____ of jail last night.
3 Can you cross milk _____ the shopping list? I bought some last night.
4 Could I book _____ to my room, please? My name is Mr Black.
5 Terrible rain today! It's absolutely pouring _____.

C Organising phrasal verbs by *topic area*

The best way to remember phrasal verbs is to organise them according to topics.

1 The phrasal verbs in the box appear in a letter from a girl to her friend. What is it about?

> break down   cheat on sb   come on to sb
> fall for sb   fall out (with sb)
> get off with sb   get on (well) with sb
> split up (with sb)

2 Read the letter and check your prediction.

Hi Ali,
Guess what's happened! Emma phoned me up last night – we were chatting away for a while and then all of a sudden she [1]_____ and started crying. I asked her what the matter was. It turns out she and Jake [2]_____! Things hadn't been going well between them, Emma said, and they [3]_____ again at the weekend when she accused him of [4]_____ her. I tried to say the normal stuff to cheer her up, you know, but the thing is, well, Jake has been cheating on her – with me! I feel terrible, but I just don't know what to do – she's my best friend! You know how I've always [5]_____ Jake really well? Well, I bumped into him a couple of weeks ago in Revolution, that new bar on George Street. We got chatting and he started [6]_____ me. I know I shouldn't have done it, but in the end we [7]_____ each other, and now I don't know what to do. I think I [8]_____ him, Ali, but I really don't want to hurt Emma! What am I going to do?
Love Chloe

3 Complete the letter using an appropriate form of the phrasal verbs in the box.

4 List phrasal verbs related to the topic of clothes.

5 Clubs

Language focus

Overview of passive forms

1 Put the words in order to make complete sentences.

1 future generations / the benefit / the environment / to be / is important / for / of / protected / for

It <u>is important for the environment to be protected for the benefit of future generations.</u>

2 a later age / life expectancy / people / be / increases / at / to retire / made / should

As _____

_____

3 being / defence / rather than / government money / health and education / much / is / on / on / spent

Too _____

_____

4 higher taxes / the money / used sensibly / to pay / if / wouldn't mind / they knew / be / being / would / forced

People _____

_____

5 enough exercise / the need / being / to look after / still / don't / about / we / warned / do / ourselves

Despite _____

_____

6 recognised / the right / a private life / enjoy / many celebrities / they / being / still have / to

Although _____

_____

7 in the future / a bilingual household / to learn / brought up / in / easier / other languages / who / will find / are / it

Children _____

_____

8 24 hours a day / an increase / will inevitably / sold / lead to / violent crime / alcohol / to be / in

Allowing _____

_____

2 Complete each sentence with the correct form of the verb provided.

1 My grandmother lives in a very old house. (build)
It <u>was built</u> more than 200 years ago and has been in our family ever since.

2 Drinking and driving is a very serious problem in many countries. (cause)
It _____ thousands of accidents every year.

3 The Minister is under pressure to resign as a result of the scandal. (hold)
He _____ a press conference later this morning.

4 Heathrow Airport will remain closed this morning as a result of the bad weather. (cancel)
Hundreds of flights _____ already, and further cancellations are likely later today.

5 The volcano is increasingly unstable, and an eruption is thought to be imminent. (move)
Thousands of people _____ out of the area by troops over the next few days, as a precautionary measure.

6 The final of the 200 metres was one of the closest races ever seen in the Olympics. (declare)
After a photo finish, Young _____ the winner by less than 0.02 of a second.

7 Train services have been delayed as a result of a security alert. (raise)
The alarm _____ when a passenger noticed a suspicious package under a seat.

8 As usual the hospital was understaffed. (keep)
In the end we _____ waiting nearly three hours before the doctor saw us.

3 Complete the two newspaper stories with the correct form of the verbs in brackets.

Text 1

A man who shot his own car ¹ __has been jailed__ (jail) for two months after ² _____ (find) guilty of discharging a firearm in public. Jack McGarvey, 64, ³ _____ (see) by a neighbour as he fired five rounds into the engine of his car around dusk on Tuesday 17ᵗʰ March, and the police ⁴ _____ (call) to the scene. It is believed that he lost his temper when his car failed to start. In court, McGarvey was said to have become increasingly aggressive and unstable since ⁵ _____ (fire) from his job as, ironically, a car mechanic. It is the fourth gun-related crime to have been committed in the area in the last month.

Text 2

Guests at a private party in a luxury hotel ⁶ _____ (take) aback on ⁷ _____ (offer) cannabis as well as the traditional after-dinner cigar at the end of their meal, it was reported yesterday. As the guests were all off-duty police officers celebrating the retirement of their boss, it was not long before an arrest ⁸ _____ (make), and the unlucky dealer ⁹ _____ (lead) away to spend a long night in the cells of the local police station. The 17-year-old, who ¹⁰ _____ (not name), is assumed to have been unaware of the identity of the guests. He has been released on police bail.

Distancing devices

1 Read the first sentence of a radio news report of the first story. Circle two factual differences between the report and text 1.

Former policeman, Jack McGarvey, was today sentenced to spend the next two years in jail after being found guilty of discharging a firearm in public.

2 (5.1) Listen to the complete report and circle six more differences in text 1.

3 Listen again and put the distancing devices in the order in which you hear them. One of them is not used.

a) is reported to have been seen _____

b) there is a general feeling _____

c) it appears _____

d) It has not been revealed _____

e) It would seem that __1__

f) here is a sense of shock _____

g) which it is now known _____

Quantifiers with & without *of*

Read the description of the Crips street gang. In which of the underlined quantifiers is the word *of* required?

¹ One of the most infamous street gangs in the world, the Los Angeles Crips, was founded by Raymond Washington and Stanley 'Tookie' Williams in 1969. Originally called the Avenue Babies, the gang eventually became known as the Westside Crips, the name 'Crips' being first used after ² several of the gang's victims reported being attacked by groups of youths, ³ all of whom wore blue bandanas and carried canes as if they were crippled. The name stuck, although in recent years ⁴ most of their members have stopped wearing bandanas since they drew ⁵ too much of attention from the police. The Crips became popular throughout southern Los Angeles as ⁶ more and more of gangs joined. ⁷ Some of the most notorious Crip gangs include the Rollin' 60 Crips and the South Side Compton Crips, with the latter blamed for the murder of rapper Tupac Shakur in 1996. In fact, ⁸ many of the most famous rap artists in America are affiliated to either the Crips or their rivals, the Bloods – Snoop Dogg and Eazy-E being ⁹ two of – although ¹⁰ none of have been formally recognised as members by the gangs themselves.

1	one of ✓	6	_____
2	_____	7	_____
3	_____	8	_____
4	_____	9	_____
5	_____	10	_____

Vocabulary

Collective nouns for people

1 Complete the sentences using the correct collective noun.

> audience   clique   ~~club~~   crew   crowd
> gang   mob   outfit   public
> set   staff   tribes

1 It's a private __club__, so it's almost impossible to join without contacts.

2 A violent _____ protested against the arrest outside the police station.

3 I invited a _____ of close friends to my birthday party.

4 After the match, the _____ ran on to the pitch to congratulate the players.

5 All the passengers, pilots and _____ were killed in the air crash.

6 The _____ have a right to know what politicians are doing with their tax payments.

7 He and his friends are part of a _____, and they're really unfriendly to people who are not in this group.

8 Some members of the _____ walked out after the first act of the opera.

9 Police are searching for an armed _____ who have robbed various banks in the area.

10 They started from nothing, but the two brothers have now formed a very impressive professional _____.

11 Only two members of _____ broke the strike and went to work.

12 Punks, goths and rockers are examples of fashion _____.

2 Which three collective nouns often have a negative connotation? Match the words to the definitions.

1 _____: a large crowd that may be difficult to control.

2 _____: a group of criminals or a group of young people who cause trouble. Can also be used informally, with neutral connotation, to refer to a group of friends.

3 _____: a small, closed group of people who are unfriendly to others.

3 Which six collective nouns are used with the word *member*?

A member of the __audience__ / _____ /
_____ / _____ / _____ / _____

4 Which collective noun can be used in these examples?

A _____ of tools / dishes / tests / rules / keys / ideas.

Collective nouns for things

Complete the gaps to form common collocations.

> barrage   box   bunch   pile / heap   series   stack

1 We have encountered a _____ of problems.

2 There was a _____ of books and papers on the desk.

3 She received a _____ of complaints, questions and criticisms.

4 We had to move a _____ of tables and chairs from one room to another.

5 Get her a _____ of flowers or a _____ of chocolates if you can't think of a better present.

Collocations with *party*

Complete the gaps using expressions with the word *party*.

> party animal   party piece   party-pooper
> throw a party   (to) party

1 You're such a _____; how come you're always going home early?

2 It's a great city. You can _____ all night long without it costing you a fortune.

3 We'll do our _____ if you like; we sing all the ABBA tunes in Spanish. It's really funny!

4 Surely you're going to _____ for your 40th birthday, aren't you?

5 I was a real _____ when I was younger, but I'm getting too old for all of that now.

💿 **Describing things with like / as:** Try the interactive activity for this topic on your CD-ROM. **29**

Verbs & nouns

1 Which of these words are nouns and which are both nouns and verbs?

> ~~bar~~ beat crowd disco DJ (deejay)
> groove leisure noise rave rhythm scene
> soul sound style techno

Nouns	Nouns & verbs
	bar

2 Complete the gaps with the eight verbs from Exercise 1.

1 My cousin _____ at my birthday party, he played really good music.

2 The critics are _____ about that new show, they think it's great.

3 I had my hair _____ this afternoon for the party. What do you think?

4 The bouncers _____ them from entering the disco because they were wearing trainers.

5 Jake _____ the drums as if his life depended on it.

6 When the music started, everyone _____ around and started dancing together.

7 You can move and _____ to the music; you know, move your body in time with the beat.

8 That record _____ like it should be a big hit in Ibiza this year.

Listening

Football club rivalries

1 Where are these football clubs from? Match each shield (a–h) to the club names (1–8).

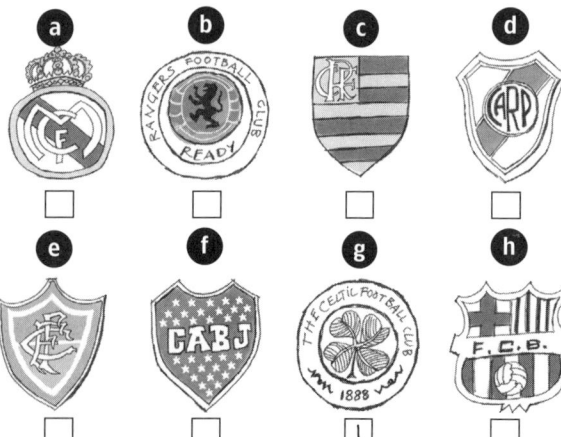

1 Celtic __from Glasgow, Scotland (g)__

2 Real Madrid _____

3 Boca Juniors _____

4 Flamengo _____

5 River Plate _____

6 Barcelona _____

7 Fluminense _____

8 Rangers _____

2a (5.2) Listen to a radio programme about the eight football clubs. Match each statement with one club from each pair.

1 Many _____ supporters were immigrants from another country.

2 _____ have beaten their rival on more occasions.

3 _____ have become a much more famous club than their rival.

4 In 2000 a _____ player signed to the rival team.

b In which country / city does each team play? Check your answers to Exercise 1.

c Which rivalry is the odd one out? Why?

_____

3 Listen again. Complete the gaps with a suitable word or expression.

1 The rivalry between Celtic and Rangers is fundamentally _____.

2 It is the _____ football rivalry in Britain.

3 Argentinian fans _____ a lot when they watch a match.

4 Unfortunately, the Argentine derby is occasionally marked by _____.

5 The Brazilian rivalry started life as a / an _____ about money.

6 Flamengo are now considered the _____ in Brazil.

7 The Spanish derby is often considered more important than watching _____ play.

8 Luis Figo received an angry _____ from Barcelona fans when he signed for Real Madrid, their arch-rivals.

ZOOM IN: *beat*

1 Look at these two examples of *beat*. What does *beat* mean in each example?

a) *Jake beat the drums as if his life depended on it.*

b) *Boca Juniors have beaten their rival on more occasions.*

2 Provide a synonym for each example of *beat*.

1 I bet you can't *beat* me in the exam.

2 *Beat* the eggs together and then add milk and a little salt.

3 I was so shocked; my heart seemed to *beat* faster.

4 He *was* badly *beaten up* by the home fans.

5 We *beat* the deadline, now we can relax!

6 I try to leave home early in the morning to *beat* the rush-hour traffic.

3 Complete the gaps with a suitable expression with *beat* from the diagram.

beat about the bush   you can't beat it!

beat the system   (**beat**)   it beats me (*inf*)

beat it (*inf*)

1 Fiddling your tax return is an easy way to _____.

2 Just _____! Leave me alone!

3 Being on holiday is great, isn't it? I mean _____, can you?

4 Stop _____ and tell me what's on your mind.

5 _____ how he got that job in the first place, he's completely incompetent.

Guided writing: *Minutes of a meeting*

1 Read the agenda for a sports club Annual General Meeting (AGM). Match the underlined items to the descriptions (a−f).

Westcliffe Sports Club Annual General Meeting

Thursday 20th November 6.30–9.30
Attendees: Club Committee (President, Captain, Treasurer, Club Secretary, Junior Secretary, Membership Secretary); Club members' representatives
Chairperson: Jon Taylor (Club President)

AGENDA

1 Apologies
2 Minutes
3 Matters arising
4 Review of season – club captain
5 Junior section – report by junior secretary
6 Treasurer's report
7 Elections for new year
8 AOB
9 Next meeting

a) A summary of the previous meeting. __2__

b) Any other business. _____

c) The developments which have taken place since the last meeting. _____

d) An outline of the financial issues. _____

e) A summary of who is not able to attend the meeting with their reasons. _____

f) A review of the performance of the sports team(s) during the last season. _____

2 Match the verbs (1−10) with the collocations (a−j).

1 make	a) from voting
2 abstain	b) what was said
3 propose	c) a document
4 vote	d) a vote
5 take	e) a note of sth
6 proofread	f) information
7 submit	g) your notes
8 cross-reference	h) a motion
9 transcribe	i) for sb
10 type up	j) sth for approval

3 Read the guidelines on taking minutes. Decide which things you should do (DOs) and which you shouldn't (DON'Ts).

1 pass round an attendance sheet for people at the meeting to sign __DO__

2 make a note of who arrives late or leaves early _____

3 record events in the order they were in on the original agenda _____

4 transcribe each opinion word-for-word to make sure details are not lost _____

5 record how votes are taken (by voice, a show of hands or secret ballot) _____

6 note down what action is agreed on and who is to carry it out _____

7 add your own personal opinions where appropriate _____

8 distribute the minutes to all those who attended _____

4 (5.3) Listen to a business consultant explaining how to take minutes of a meeting. Check your answers.

5 Listen again and make a note of any other DOs and DON'Ts which are mentioned.

6 Read the extract from the Westcliffe Sports Club AGM and answer the questions.

> **Tony Davis** (Treasurer): Good evening everyone. I would like first of all to give an overview of the current financial status of the club, before outlining proposals I have for fund-raising ventures for the forthcoming year. I would welcome initial reactions from the floor to these proposals and also be delighted to hear other suggestions for ways to raise funds should anyone have any ideas.
>
> The year has been a great success from a financial point of view as well as from a sporting perspective. The number of full members has increased from 458 last year to 585, whilst the new social membership option for non-playing members has also proved a success. Thirty-six people have so far taken advantage of this option. Increased membership, along with the slight increase in fees for full members from £125 to £140, means the club is now better off than at any stage in the last five years. Full details of the club accounts will be made available to all members in the end of year report next month. Does anyone have any questions or comments at this stage? Yes, Danny Matthews.
>
> **Danny Matthews** (Member): Given that fees went up significantly last year, can we expect a further increase in the new year?
>
> **TD:** No, members will be pleased to hear that fees will remain the same for at least one more year. It has been decided that as the club appears to be financially secure for the time being, no further increase in membership fees is necessary. Er ... Paul Howe?
>
> **Paul Howe** (Member): Does the same apply to the prices of drinks in the bar?
>
> **TD:** That, I'm afraid, is something you will have to ask the bar manager. Any other questions? No? OK, moving on, then…

1 Which item on the agenda is being discussed?

2 In what ways has the club had a successful year?

3 What decision has the club committee taken for the following year?

7 Read the minutes written for this part of the meeting. How could they be improved?

> The man in charge of the club's finances then talked about how much money the club had made during the year. Apparently we've got more than a hundred extra members since last year. As the cost of joining also went up, by 15 quid, the club is better off than ever. Danny cynically asked if the membership fee would go up yet again next year – if you ask me it should come down, but I don't suppose there's much chance of that! The Junior Secretary (I can't remember his name) asked if the prices in the bar would stay the same, which got everyone laughing. I missed the answer because Philippa H came back in at that point and everyone had to stand up so she could get to her seat!

8 (5.4) Now listen to the rest of the discussion. Take notes on:

1 the names of the speakers

2 the key points each speaker makes

3 any proposals or motions which are put forward

4 the outcome of any proposals

9 Write the minutes for this part of the meeting. Refer back to the list of DOs and DON'Ts if necessary.

1 Test yourself!

Reading

(20 marks)

1 Read an interview with author Malcolm Gladwell about his book *Blink*. Match the interviewer's questions with the answers. (_____ / 4)

a) What effect would you like *Blink* to have on its readers?

b) Where did you get the idea for *Blink*?

c) How can thinking that takes place so quickly be useful?

d) ~~What is *Blink* about?~~

e) Does *Blink* talk about when rapid cognition goes awry?

---

1 d)

When you meet someone for the first time, your mind takes about two seconds to jump to a series of conclusions. *Blink* is a book about those two seconds, because I think those instant conclusions are really powerful. It's thinking – it's just thinking that moves faster and operates more mysteriously than conscious decision making. I discuss, among other things, marriage, code-breaking, sculpture, Tom Hanks, speed-dating, how to hit a topspin forehand, and what you can learn from someone by looking around their bedroom. So what does that make *Blink*? Fun, I hope.

2 _____

We live in a society dedicated to the idea that we're better off spending as much time as possible in deliberation. But I don't think this is true. There are lots of situations – particularly at times of stress – when snap judgements offer a much better means of making sense of the world. There's a wonderful phrase in psychology – 'the power of thin slicing' – which says that as human beings we are capable of making sense of situations based on the thinnest slice of experience.

3 _____

I decided, a few years ago, to grow my hair long. And one day, a police van pulled up and three officers jumped out. They were looking for a rapist, and the rapist, they said, looked a lot like me. They pulled out the sketch and description. I pointed out to them that in fact the rapist looked nothing like me. All we had in common was curly hair. Something about the first impression created by my hair exerted a powerful hold over the officers' thinking. That episode got me thinking about the weird power of first impressions.

4 _____

That's a big part of the book. I'm very interested in situations where we need to be careful with our powers of rapid cognition. There is no correlation between height and the ability to motivate and lead people. But for some reason corporations overwhelmingly choose tall people for leadership roles. I think that's an example of bad rapid cognition: there is something going on in the first few seconds of meeting a tall person which makes us predisposed toward thinking of that person as an effective leader. With *Blink*, I'm trying to help people distinguish their good rapid cognition from their bad rapid cognition.

5 _____

It is concerned with those instantaneous impressions that bubble up whenever we have to make a decision under conditions of stress. I think it's time we paid more attention to those fleeting moments. I think that if we did, it would change the way wars are fought, the kind of products we see on the shelves, the way job interviews are conducted and on and on...

---

2 Decide if the following sentences are true (T) or false (F). (_____ / 6)

1 Some forms of thinking are less well understood than others. T / F

2 Malcolm Gladwell believes that the majority of decisions require careful deliberation beforehand. T / F

3 The police stopped Malcolm Gladwell because of his strong physical resemblance to the man they were looking for. T / F

4 Many companies have decided to use rapid cognition as a way of selecting their employees. T / F

5 Companies can sometimes be deceived into associating height with management skills. T / F

6 Malcolm Gladwell believes that we do not use our powers of rapid cognition as much as we should. T / F

3 Choose the *incorrect* option in each case. (_____ / 4)

1 The book suggests that we **don't have to / shouldn't / mustn't** automatically assume that the best decisions are always the result of careful deliberation.

2 If Malcolm Gladwell hadn't been stopped by the police, he **wouldn't / needn't / mightn't** have decided to write *Blink*.

3 If we always rely on rapid cognition we **can't / might / could** make errors of judgement from time to time.

4 People **should / ought to / need** take more notice of the instant impressions they have in stressful situations.

4 Complete the sentences using passive forms of the verbs in brackets. (_____ / 6)

1 *Blink* (say) _____ to be a fun book.

2 Thin slices of experiences can be sufficient for sense (make) _____ of the world.

3 Malcolm Gladwell decided to write *Blink* after (stop) _____ by the police.

4 Many tall people might not (choose) _____ for leadership positions if companies had been more aware of how rapid cognition works.

5 More attention should (pay) _____ to moments when instant impressions are formed.

6 With only a few small changes (make) _____ to the way we use our powers of rapid cognition, the world could become a better place.

Listening

(20 marks)

1 (TY.1) Listen to a radio programme about bullying at work and order the statements. (_____ / 7)

a) The effects of bullying. _____
b) Examples of types of bullying. _____
c) Ways to deal with bullying. _____
d) Victims of bullying. _____
e) The causes of bullying. _____
f) Figures relating to workplace bullying. _____
g) Differences between different employment sectors. _____

2 Listen again and decide if the following sentences are true (T) or false (F). (_____ / 8)

1 It is usually very obvious when bullying is taking place in a company. T / F

2 Nearly a quarter of UK employees will be the victims of bullying during their working lives. T / F

3 Workplace bullying has serious economic consequences as well as psychological ones. T / F

4 Workplace bullying is equally common in all sectors of employment. T / F

5 Senior employees are more likely to bully their junior colleagues than vice versa. T / F

6 Many employees have competitions to see who can be the best bully. T / F

7 People are not always aware that they are the victims of workplace bullying. T / F

8 People are likely to be unsympathetic towards victims of bullying who are not very good at their jobs. T / F

3 Reorder the phrases to make complete sentences summarising points from the interview. (_____ / 5)

1 bullying in the workplace / what is clear is / a very serious problem / that / is now

2 of your experiences as a victim of bullying / by keeping / make it easier / you will / for people outside the company / to help you / a written record

3 although / it does / bullying occurs / appear / more common / in those sectors where people are / in all employment sectors, / to be / under more pressure

4 not always obvious / bullying / when / is taking place / the fact is, / in work environments / it is

5 you are not doing / no reason at all / there is / that if / it is because / you are being bullied / your job / well / to think

Writing

(15 marks)

You have begun to feel concerned about your relationship with either your partner or a work colleague.
Write a letter to your partner or an e-mail to your colleague expressing your concerns. Include the following:

1 A description of the problem as you see it.

2 Possible causes of the problem.

3 Suggestions for what action could be taken to resolve the situation.

Language Passport

Self-assessment grid

- Use this checklist to identify what you **can do** after completion of the three preceding units, as well as to identify your own language-learning **priorities.**
- Use the right-hand column as a reference to where you can find **more help.**

Units 1–5			I can do this	This is a priority	For more help
Understanding	**Listening**	I can follow extended speech even when it is not clearly structured and when relationships are only implied.	☐	☐	Unit 1, SB, pp. 7 & 11. Unit 2, SB, p. 15. Unit 3, SB, pp. 24–25. Unit 4, SB, pp. 37 & 38. Flashback 1, SB, pp. 50 & 53.
		I can understand lectures, talks and reports.	☐	☐	Unit 1, SB, p. 8. Unit 2, SB, pp. 17, 21. Unit 3, SB, p. 35.
		I can understand a range of idiomatic expressions and colloquialisms, appreciating shifts in style and register.	☐	☐	Unit 1, SB, pp. 8–9 & 11. Unit 2, SB, pp. 15 & 19. World English 1, SB, p. 22. Unit 3, SB, pp. 24 & 31. Unit 4, SB, p. 33. Unit 5, SB, pp. 42 & 49. Flashback 1, SB, pp. 50 & 53.
	Reading	I can understand fairly long demanding texts and summarise them orally.	☐	☐	Unit 1, SB, pp. 6–7 & 10. Unit 2, SB, pp. 17 & 20. Unit 5, SB, pp. 43, 44–5 & 46.
		I can read any correspondence with occasional use of a dictionary.	☐	☐	Unit 1, SB, p. 12.
		I can read contemporary literary texts (a poem) with ease.	☐	☐	Unit 3, SB, p. 27.
		I can recognise the social, political or historical background of a literary work.	☐	☐	Unit 3, SB, p. 27.
		I can read reports, analyses and commentaries where opinions, viewpoints and connections are discussed.	☐	☐	Unit 4, SB, p. 36.
Speaking	**Spoken Interaction**	I can keep up with an animated conversation between native speakers.	☐	☐	Unit 1, SB, pp. 10 & 13. Unit 2, SB, p. 19. Unit 3, pp. 26 & 31. Unit 4, SB, p. 33.
		I can present my ideas and opinions clearly and precisely.	☐	☐	Unit 1, SB, pp. 9 & 11. Unit 3, SB p. 25. Unit 4, SB, p. 35. Unit 5, SB p. 45. Flashback 1, SB, p. 52.
	Spoken Production	I can give clear, detailed descriptions of complex subjects.	☐	☐	Unit 2, SB, pp. 14–16.
		I can give an extended description or account of something, integrating themes, developing particular points and concluding appropriately.	☐	☐	Unit 1, SB, p. 12. Unit 2, SB, p. 17. Unit 5, SB, pp. 48–49.
Writing	**Writing**	I can write formally correct letters, for example to complain or to take a stand in favour or against something.	☐	☐	Unit 1, SB, p. 13. Guided Writing, WB, p. 8. Flashback 1, SB, p. 52.
		I can select a style appropriate to the reader in mind.	☐	☐	Unit 2, SB, p. 21. Unit 3, SB, pp. 31 & 35. Guided Writing, WB, p. 20. Unit 5, SB, p. 47.
		I can present points of view on a topic, underlining the main ideas and supporting my reasoning with detailed examples.	☐	☐	Flashback 1, SB, p. 52.

Children

Language focus

Present & past habits

1 Read the opinions about five aspects of childhood. Match them to the topics.

> a) sport   b) education   c) health   d) family   e) discipline

① Twenty years ago kids 1 **were / would be / used to be** much fitter because they had much more active lifestyles. Kids these days 2 **spend / spent / will spend** all their free time playing with their PlayStations or X-Boxes when they should be outside getting exercise in the fresh air. That's why they're always picking up illnesses and having to have days off school – they've got no resistance to germs. Topic _____

② Schools nowadays 3 **will discourage / use to discourage / discourage** competitive sports because they believe taking part is more important than winning. To me this is wrong, because competition is part of life. People are 4 **always / ever / forever** trying to beat or outdo each other, and schools should prepare children for this aspect of the real world. What better place to do this than on the playing fields? Topic _____

④ People 7 **are always going on / use to go on / will go on** about how today's kids waste their time using computers, but for me computers, through the internet, online forums and weblogs, provide all sorts of educational opportunities which previous generations 8 **didn't use to have / wouldn't have / didn't have**, and children should be encouraged to use them as much as possible. Topic _____

③ In the old days kids who were naughty 5 **will / would / used to** get a smack around the ear from their mum or dad. Now parents 6 **don't / don't use to / won't** so much as lay a finger on their children for fear of being accused of child abuse, and as a result children themselves have no respect for authority. They get away with all sorts of behaviour which was unheard of in my day. Topic _____

⑤ It's much better to be an only child, because brothers and sisters 9 **are forever having / would have / have** to share things whereas an only child gets everything! When I was growing up my two cousins 10 **would waste / were wasting / used to waste** their time fighting with each other, while I was always off having fun with my mates! And I got lots more presents on my birthday! Topic _____

2 Which *two* ways of talking about present or past habits are possible in each case? Circle the correct answers.

3 Read the e-mail. What was Caron's reason for writing it? _____

E-mail

| File | Print | Send | Attach | Reply | Forward | Cancel | Address |

Hi Judy,

I know you've got a lot on your plate at the moment, but I need a bit of advice about Laura. Basically she's been acting really strangely lately, not just with me but at school as well. The other day I got a letter from them saying she's been missing classes, which I can't understand 'cos she never 1 _used_ 2 _____ miss school, even when she was ill! The school's really strict about attendance; kids are 3 _____ 4 _____ suspended for skipping classes, and that's the last thing we need with L's exams coming up. It's not just that, though. She's completely changed the way she is with people; her teachers, her friends, everyone. Before 5 _____ 6 _____ put her hand up before anyone else when the teacher asked them a question and she 7 _____ 8 _____ get brilliant reports for all her subjects, but now she's just stopped trying. And apparently she 9 _____ 10 _____ swearing and answering back. I know we used 11 _____ 12 _____ a bit cheeky when we were in our teens and 13 _____ 14 _____ always getting up to something, but we 15 _____ 16 _____ to be that bad, did we? To be honest, I think there's something else going on. 17 _____ 18 _____ always hanging around with those kids from one of the rough estates, for a start. She comes home in the afternoon, has a quick shower and then she 19 _____ 20 _____ out until all hours. I can't imagine what they get up to! Anyway, what do you think I should do? Any suggestions?

Caron

---

4 Complete the e-mail using the words in the box.

> always (x2)   be   being   didn't   is (x2)
> she (x2)   stay   to (x3)   use   used (x2)
> we   were   will   would

Spoken narrative techniques

1 Read the extracts from a childhood 'naughty story' and guess what happened.

  1 I must have been about five or six… _____

  2 my dad used to be a teacher _____

  3 although I was only very young, I obviously had an artistic streak in me. _____

  4 this particular day my dad was away _____

  5 I must have thought my latest art project was going to be too much for me on my own _____

  6 having already painted the door and the path, I needed a new challenge _____

2 (6.1) Listen to the first part of the story. Which discourse marker is used before each extract (1–6) *well*, *anyway* or *so*?

3 Match the two parts of the extracts.

  1 …he used to go away for a week on these _f_

  2 …it became this _____

  3 My dad always kept these _____

  4 …I would think, _____

  5 …my dad was away on one of these _____

  6 She said something like, _____

  7 I had this _____

  8 …digging around in all this _____

  a) 'Go and play outside for a while so Mummy can look after your sister.'

  b) DIY stuff

  c) old pots of paints and old paintbrushes

  d) friend who lived along the road

  e) camping trips

  f) camping holidays with his school

  g) annual family holiday

  h) 'Right, what can I paint today?'

4 Listen again and check your answers. What do you think happened next?

5 Underline examples of the following in Transcript 6.1.

  1 *this* or *these* used instead of *a, the,* or *some* to make the story more immediate

  2 use of reporting verbs followed by direct speech

  3 use of the spoken discourse markers *so, anyway,* and *well*

6 Read the second part of the story and see if you were correct.

> Right in front of our eyes, gleaming in the sunshine on the driveway, was my dad's brand new car. And the next minute, there we were, happily painting the car, well, all the colours of the rainbow. I was a bit too young to remember it myself, ¹_e_! Anyway, we'd managed to paint one side of the car when this neighbour spotted us. So he knocked on our door and when my mum answered, holding my sister, ²___, he was like, 'Sorry to bother you Isobel, but you do realise your son and his friend are painting your new car, don't you?' So my mum ran out of the house, saw what we'd done, and went absolutely ballistic! ³___, but I'm sure they weren't words that two five-year-olds should hear. And to make matters worse, my friend's dad and another neighbour had heard the commotion in the street ⁴___, and as soon as they saw what we'd done, instead of helping my mum, they fell about laughing!
>
> Picture the scene. My mum screaming at us; my sister crying at the top of her voice; these two fully-grown adults rolling around in hysterical laughter; my friend and I standing there with our paintbrushes ⁵___; and this brand new car looking like something Picasso might have come up with! Anyway, we did the only logical thing; we ran away! My mum obviously couldn't run after us with my baby sister, so in no time at all we had disappeared. Once she'd calmed down a bit, my mum realised that it wasn't really a good idea for two terrified kids to be running around near a busy road so she started panicking, ⁶___ and she would be left with this terrible guilt. So I think she probably left my sister with a neighbour and set off to look for us.
>
> Well, I don't know how long we were, let's say, 'on the run' for; probably until teatime. According to my mum she looked all over the neighbourhood ⁷___, before she eventually found us hiding behind a postbox. She was, 'Oh, I'm so happy you're both OK. Don't you ever run off like that again, however frightened you are!' In fact she was so relieved to find us that we got away without any punishment whatsoever. Well, apart from a couple of hours scrubbing the car with soap and water, that is!

7 Complete the story using the extracts below. One of the extracts is not used.

  a) I don't know what her exact words were

  b) which was something I'd never tried before

  c) and was getting more and more frantic with worry

  d) and came out to see what was happening

  e) but according to my mum it was quite a sight

  f) wondering what all the fuss was about

  g) who was still shrieking at the top of her voice

  h) thinking that we were going to get hit by a car

8 (6.2) Listen and check your answers.

Vocabulary

Word-building: Adjectives

Complete the sentences with the correct form of the word in brackets.

1 He can't bear losing. Most middle children have a very _competitive_ attitude. (compete).

2 He was always trying to chat up the girls even as a kid. He was very _____ even then. (flirt)

3 As you get older, you get more _____. You start to believe in yourself more. (confidence)

4 Oldest children are often the most _____ because they have to create a good impression. (sense)

5 On the other hand, the youngest child is likely to be the most _____, if only to attract attention to themselves. (rebel)

6 If you're an only child, you have no choice but to be _____. (depend)

7 Youngest children are more likely to be _____. (manipulate)

8 That film was a _____ look at child rearing; it wasn't trying to be serious. (heart)

Personality phrases

1 Complete each phrase with one of the words.

> control   co-operative   fussy   overindulged
> laugh   loner   sulky   ~~the show~~

1 A: She's really bossy, isn't she?
   B: Yeah, she certainly loves running _the show_, that's for sure.

2 A: He's the typical youngest son, so spoilt!
   B: I know, they are usually really _____, aren't they?

3 A: She doesn't mind being on her own, does she?
   B: No, deep down she's a real _____.

4 A: He seems to get on with his parents, doesn't he?
   B: Oh yeah, he's very _____; he even helps his mum in the kitchen!

5 A: I think he's so funny.
   B: Absolutely, he's a real _____ at parties.

6 A: She really worries about little things all the time.
   B: I know, it's infuriating, she's so _____.

7 A: He seems depressed. He won't talk to me.
   B: I know, my son's the same; he's just so _____ sometimes.

8 A: He gets these tantrums; I don't know what to do about it.
   B: I know. It's like he gets out of _____, and then it just passes.

2 (6.3) Listen and check.

3 Which of the expressions have negative connotations? Are the others positive or neutral?

Negative	Positive	Neutral
sulky		

Describing characteristic behaviour and habits: Try the interactive activity for this topic on your CD-ROM.

Politically correct language

What is another way of saying these politically correct phrases?

Physical difficulties

a) visually impaired _____blind_____

b) hearing impaired _____

c) physically challenged _____

Jobs and positions

d) chair person _____

e) police officer _____

f) flight attendant _____

g) between jobs _____

Ethnic groups

h) African-American _____

i) Native American _____

j) Inuit _____

People and relationships

k) spouse _____

l) gender _____

m) Ms Smith _____

Vocabulary extension

Sexist language

1 A number of idioms refer to the stereotypical portrayal of men in society. Match the expressions (1–6) with the meanings (a–f).

1 He's a man of the world.

2 Are you man enough for this job?

3 He's a good family man.

4 It's a shame, he's just become another of those men in suits.

5 He likes to be one of the lads.

6 He really is his own man; he never follows rules.

a) a responsible father

b) a member of a group

c) a man who has seen life

d) a man who conforms to a certain lifestyle

e) an independent man

f) sufficiently strong / brave

2 Do you think of any of the expressions can also refer to the female sex?

3 Underline any sexist language in these sentences and replace it with an appropriate alternative.

1 Walking on the moon was a 'giant step for <u>mankind</u>'. _humankind_

2 That's made of man-made fibres. _____

3 'If you misbehave again, you'll go straight to the headmaster'. _____

4 'There's a sign that says "barmaids required", you could always apply.' _____

5 I'm hopeless with my hands. I'll have to get a man in to fix the sink. _____

6 We appointed Mark as chairman of the meeting, as he's the most sensible. _____

Paraphrasing is a communication strategy which we use if 1) we don't know the exact word or phrase that we want to use, 2) the listener doesn't understand us or 3) saying the word would be too direct or hurtful.

1 Read the dialogues. Which word or idea is being paraphrased by the phrases in bold?

1

A: How's your son getting on at school these days?

B: Well, you know he finds it a little hard to keep up sometimes. He's having some, you know … **trouble following the class.** You know he might have to go to … **special classes** soon to help him out, a bit.

A: Oh, I see what you mean.

B: I think it's quite normal, though.

2

A: Now, your daughter is making excellent progress. But she does **keep herself to herself.** Is she like that at home?

B: Well, no, actually, she's not like that at all. I think she finds it hard to … **to come out of her shell** with people she doesn't know. You know she's a bit…

A: Yes, well, that's quite common at that age, she's sure to get more sociable in time.

3

A: He's a good child, of course he is, but he won't go anywhere without his mother.

B: Oh, I know at that age it's a bit worrying, he's always, you know … **hanging on her every word,** he won't **take,** you know … **take the initiative.**

A: Yes, well, the youngest son's often like that, of course.

2 Which adjectives could describe the child in each conversation, but might be too direct?

1 *unintelligent,*_____

2 _____

3 _____

3 How could you paraphrase the following descriptions of children?

1 He's so **naughty** at home, but **well-behaved** in class.

2 She's very **vague** and **indecisive** about what she wants.

3 He's very **spoilt** and **demanding.**

4 🔊(6.4) Listen to three dialogues. Note the way the adjectives in Exercise 3 are paraphrased.

a) naughty *slightly out of control*_____

b) well-behaved _____

c) vague _____

d) indecisive _____

e) spoilt _____

f) demanding _____

5 Using understatement is a common way of paraphrasing. Does it strengthen or reduce the effect of the original adjective?

6 🔊(6.5) Listen to six extracts. What is each person talking about?

	Topic	Understatement
1	food	a little bit hot
2		
3		
4		
5		
6		

7 Listen again. Write the understatement next to the topic in Exercise 6.

8 Write your own examples of understatement for each phrase.

1 The food is disgusting. _____
_____

2 He's completely drunk. _____
_____

3 The meal was really expensive. _____
_____

We use politically correct language to avoid offending specific social groups, particularly those identified by religion, ethnic background, gender, employment or physical status.

1 Match these politically incorrect terms with their politically correct equivalents.

1 girlfriend/boyfriend	a) winter break
2 unemployment benefit	b) partner
3 dinner lady	c) with learning difficulties
4 educationally subnormal	d) international students
5 foreign students	e) jobseeker's allowance
6 Christmas holiday	f) meals assistant

2 Each pair below shows two ways of expressing similar information. Tick (✓) the option you think is more politically correct in each case.

1 a) 100 members of the public were asked how domestic chores should be shared.
   b) 100 members of the public, 67 of them female and 33 male, were asked how domestic chores should be shared.

2 a) Many epileptics need to take daily medication.
   b) Many people with epilepsy need to take daily medication.

3 a) A person who has had a stroke often experiences partial paralysis.
   b) A stroke victim often experiences partial paralysis.

4 a) My dad is confined to a wheelchair.
   b) My dad uses a wheelchair.

5 a) My friend works as a nurse at the hospital.
   b) My friend works as a male nurse at the hospital.

6 a) We're going to get a new boss. I hope he's nice!
   b) We're going to get a new boss, who I hope is nice.

7 a) The guests were shouting and swearing in a rude and impolite way which was socially unacceptable.
   b) The guests were shouting and swearing in a very unladylike way.

8 a) Dear Sir,
   b) Dear Head of Studies,

3 Match the explanations with the sentences in Exercise 2.

a) Emphasise people's abilities rather than their limitations. __4__

b) Define and describe human groups as fully as possible in terms of gender or race. ____

c) Avoid using words which are gender-specific even if the alternative is less concise. ____

d) Use emotionally neutral language which does not have negative connotations. ____

e) Do not label people by their disabilities. The person and the disability should be kept separate. ____

f) If the gender of the recipient of a formal letter is unknown, address the person by their job title rather than *Dear Sir* or *Dear Madam*. ____

g) Avoid qualifying job titles unnecessarily by using gender-specific adjectives such as male and female, since this reinforces outdated gender stereotypes. ____

h) Do not assume the gender of an employee in a job which is not gender-specific, even when this job is or has been typically dominated by one gender. ____

4 Rewrite these sentences in a more politically correct way.

1 There are currently a number of Arab students studying in the school.
   <u>The school currently has students from Libya,</u>
   <u>Egypt, Kuwait, Saudi Arabia and Iran.</u>

2 Amputees sometimes feel self-conscious in public.

3 Spring can be an uncomfortable time for asthma sufferers.

4 She has been partially blind since she was born.

5 Our new MP is a retired female judge.

6 The most important quality in a secretary is that she should be organised.

7 My cousins are real career women.

8 The Editor, Evening News, Dear Sir or Madam,

Language focus

Regrets

1 Match the people with the past events or decisions they regret.

1 Over the years we've spent a fortune on rent with nothing to show for it. __a__

2 She always has to rely on friends or public transport to get around. _____

3 He created a bad impression and, as a result, didn't get the job. _____

4 They were late getting to the airport, and missed their flight. _____

5 I couldn't go to my best friend's wedding. _____

6 The lies told by the alleged victim during the trial led to the defendant's conviction. _____

a) ~~not buying a house~~

b) giving false evidence

c) getting caught in rush-hour traffic

d) not learning to drive

e) arriving late for an interview

f) being in hospital for an operation

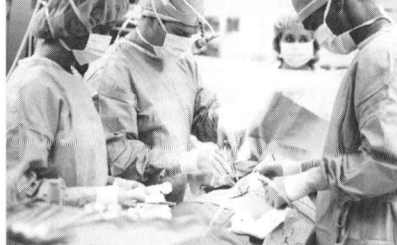

2 Write sentences expressing the regrets of the people in Exercise 1.

1 We ... wish / buy / a house / five years ago / when / have / enough money / in / bank.
We wish we had bought a house five years ago when we had enough money in the bank.

2 She ... regret / not learn / to drive / when / be / younger.

_____

3 If ... car / break down / on / way / to / station / not / arrive / late / the interview.

_____

4 They ... should / leave / earlier / in / afternoon / to avoid / rush hour.

_____

5 I ... love / be able / go / her wedding.

_____

6 Had ... alleged victim / tell / truth / the defendant / never / be / convicted.

_____

3 Find and correct the mistake in each of the sentences.

1 I wish I studied a bit harder when I was at school.

_____

2 I regret have too much to drink last night!

_____

3 I'm so sleepy. I shouldn't had had such a big lunch.

_____

4 I would like have started studying English at an earlier age.

_____

5 Have I done more exercise in the past I would be fitter now.

_____

The past with present or future meaning

1 Match the sentences with the pictures.

2 Now write similar sentences for these pictures.

1 I wish you were here with me.
2 It's time you got up and got ready for school!
3 If we were a year older they'd let us in.
4 Supposing we took a taxi instead?
5 We'd rather you got a proper job instead.
6 I'd sooner you didn't smoke, if it's all the same to you.

1 I wish I _____
2 It's time someone _____
3 If you _____
4 Supposing we _____
5 Wouldn't you rather we _____
6 I'd sooner we _____

3 Complete the sentences to make them true for you, using the past with present or future meaning.

1 I wish _____
2 It's time _____
3 If _____
4 Supposing _____
5 I'd rather _____
6 I'd sooner _____

Vocabulary

Emotional ups & downs

1 Are the expressions positive or negative?

a) cheer sb up __positive__

b) finish sb off _____

c) freak sb out _____

d) get sb down _____

e) make sb's day _____

f) make sb mad _____

2 Complete the sentences (1–6) with one of the expressions (a–f).

1 It really _____ me up to see young people enjoying themselves.

2 Getting your letter really _____ my day, thanks a lot for taking the trouble!

3 Waiting for you in the freezing cold really _____ me off – it's always the same with you!

4 You looked so ill all of a sudden, it really _____ me out. I thought you were going to faint.

5 The winter weather always _____ me down. I can't help it.

6 It _____ me mad that sometimes we have to be polite to people who we can't stand.

Vocabulary extension

Mood swings

1 Do these expressions describe positive or negative moods?

gloomy		un a downer
fired-up		overwhelmed
over the moon	to be	on an up
on edge		the last straw

2a Which expression is used to describe a situation, not a mood?

_____

b Which could be used in both a negative and positive context?

_____

3 Complete the gaps with an appropriate expression from the diagram in Exercise 1.

1 He's really _____ at the moment, but not for long – tomorrow he'll come crashing down again!

2 When I found out that I had lost my job as well, it was really _____!

3 She's been _____ all day; I don't know what she's got to be nervous about!

4 On hearing that I'd won the prize, I was just so _____ by emotion – I didn't know whether to laugh or cry!

5 That whole month, I was _____; I just thought that I was a total failure.

6 Teenagers these days are a _____ bunch, always depressed. Don't they realise how lucky they are?

7 I'm really _____ just before I get up on stage. It's part of the excitement of a live performance.

8 When they win, footballers often say they are _____ or 'on top of the world'. These expressions have become a bit of a cliché.

Humour

1 Circle the word which does not belong to the group. Explain your choice.

1 giggle, laugh, grin, chuckle _____

2 funny, witty, hilarious, fun _____

3 pun, joke, tease, gag _____

4 sarcastic, parody, satire, irony _____

5 comedian, comic, laughter, clown _____

6 tease, make fun of, mock, snigger _____

2 Complete the sentences with words from Exercise 1. More than one answer is possible.

1 You take life too seriously; you should try to see the _____ side sometimes.

2 He had an enormous _____ on his face when I walked in, so I knew there was good news.

3 When I was at school, some of the kids _____ me for being chubby.

4 I couldn't stop _____; sometimes you get these laughing fits and can't stop.

5 The party was brilliant; we all had a real _____!

6 Groucho Marx was a great _____ actor.

7 Berlin is such a _____ city; there's so much to do there.

8 His humour is full of _____ or plays on words and too much sexual innuendo.

Hot and cold metaphors: Try the interactive activity for this topic on your CD-ROM.

Reading

Advertising techniques

1 Match the headings (a–h) to the paragraphs (1–8).

- a) Ask the Expert
- b) A Slice of Life
- c) ~~Before and After~~
- d) Association of Ideas
- e) Blinded by Science
- f) Close-ups
- g) Key words
- h) Guilt

1 __c)__

The product offers an instant and radical transformation. The sudden change is always positive and **marks** a great contrast in the life of the user. An old-fashioned but effective technique.

2 _____

Advertisers sometimes use specialist, often technical, jargon to trick customers. A product which has been laboratory tested or contains a special (and perhaps invented) ingredient may have more **cachet**.

3 _____

We often relate a certain concept to a particular product. For example, advertisers like to connect driving with freedom, space and well-being. Our status is often **enhanced** if we buy a particular product which says a lot about us and our role in society.

4 _____

Companies often encourage us to buy a product because somebody successful or with certain authority gives it their **seal of approval**. These adverts often involve a demonstration of the product's effectiveness.

5 _____

Most adverts contain **catchy** slogans or one-liners which help consumers remember a particular product. These words and phrases often conjure up positive emotions. Sometimes they become more important than the product itself.

6 _____

Ordinary people talk about a product, usually in an everyday situation or **vignette**. It is often easier for the consumer to identify with a real-life person than an expert or a star.

7 _____

Adverts often make you feel that your behaviour is **flawed** or irresponsible because you don't happen to own or use a particular product. They are often associated with products that you buy for other people.

8 _____

State-of-the-art photographic techniques are used to make a product more attractive than it is in reality. We often find that when we get the product home, it does not look half as good.

2 Explain the words in bold in your own words.

1. __signals__
2. _____
3. _____
4. _____
5. _____
6. _____
7. _____
8. _____

3 (71) Listen to five adverts. Complete the table.

Product	Consumer
1 __an iron__	_____
2 _____	_____
3 _____	_____
4 _____	_____
5 _____	_____

4 Listen again. Which techniques from the reading text are used in each advert?

ZOOM IN: *up*

1   What does this expression with *up* mean?

Our marriage has had its fair share of ups and downs.

2   Complete the sentences, using expressions from the diagram.

time is up		be up to sth
ups and downs		on the up and up
it's up to you	expressions with up	up to one's ears/neck/eyes in sth
the right/wrong way up		up-and-coming

1   I can't possibly come out tonight; I'm _____ in work.

2   I'm afraid, your _____. I need your answer now.

3   He's behaving very strangely lately, he must be _____.

4   I don't want to put any pressure on you. It's _____ what you do with your life.

5   That painting is the _____, can you change it round?

6   The government usually says that the economy is _____, but I don't believe them.

7   We've had our _____, but I think we're over the worst.

8   The Argentinian centre-forward is only 18; he's one of the _____ stars in the Barcelona team.

3   In phrasal verbs, the particle *up* has several meanings. Look at the diagram.

| a) separate into pieces | | c) move to a higher position |
| b) complete an action | phrasal verbs with up | d) improve |

Match each example of *up* with one of the meanings (a–d).

1   Can you *clean up* this mess please? _____

2   *Get up* on that chair and hand me the dictionary from the top shelf, will you? _____

3   *Cut up* the cake into smaller pieces or there won't be enough to go round. _____

4   He *wrapped up* the present beautifully. _____

5   The weather's *looking up*, isn't it? _____

6   I really *cheered up* when they announced that I had passed. _____

7   *Chop up* the wood and put it on the fire. _____

8   The sun *was coming up* over the mountains. _____

Guided writing: *A curriculum vitae*

1   Look at the example of a well-written curriculum vitae (CV). What job is the person applying for?

2   Complete the CV putting the section headings in the correct place (A–G).

1 Career Objective ____   3 Employment History ____   5 Other Skills ____   7 Professional Training ____

2 Education ____   4 Interests ____   6 Personal Profile ____   8 References ____

3   Look at the tips for writing an effective CV. Underline everything you are advised *not* to do.

4   Match the tips with the relevant, underlined parts of the CV. Not all the tips are illustrated.

5   If you were the prospective employer, would you invite this candidate for an interview? Why / not?

6   Write your CV to accompany an application for your ideal job. Use appropriate headings and refer to the tips.

Prabhat Keswani

7 Malpas Drive, Salford, Manchester, M23 1JF
Tel: (0161) 234 1234   e-mail: prabk@hotmail.com

Personal Details
Date of Birth: 17ᵗʰ July 1974
Nationality: British

A: _____
To secure a managerial position within a training department to seek new challenges and enable fellow professionals to benefit from the knowledge and skills acquired during ten years' practical experience in quality assurance.

B: _____
A senior quality assurance manager with a wide range of experience in the food industry. Excellent leadership skills, having managed a team now established as the most innovative in the industry.

C: _____

May 1999–date

Senior Quality Assurance Manager: WEBB Foods Ltd, Reading
Managing quality assurance and reporting directly to factory manager.
Managing team of six people.

Apr 1996–Dec 1998

Quality Assurance Technician: Grayson Foods Ltd, Guildford
- Creating computer applications to monitor factory environment.
- Ensuring new equipment complied with quality assurance procedures.

D: _____

Jan–Nov 2004

High Diploma in Quality Assurance: Technical Institute, Maidenhead (part-time)

Jan–Apr 1999

Team Leadership Course: Guildford College of Higher Education, Guildford

E: _____

1992–1995
1985–1992

BA Honours (Biochemistry): University of Nottingham
Ferryhouse School, Leicester
A-levels in Mathematics (Grade A), Economics (A) and Physics (B).
8 GCSEs.

F: _____
Full, clean driving licence.
First Aid Gold Certificate holder.
Experienced user of Windows NT4 and Windows 2000 operating systems.

G: _____
Playing football; motorcycling; physical fitness.

H: _____
Available on request.

Top Tips for CVs

1 Stating your nationality can save time. If you are not a citizen of the country where you want to work, there may be visa implications.

2 List previous relevant jobs in reverse chronological order, with dates and concise details of your responsibilities and achievements.

3 If there are gaps between periods of employment, explain what you were doing in that time, for example travelling, studying, or charity fund-raising work.

4 Do not list all your initial qualifications from school; level and number of qualifications is sufficient. List higher level qualifications by subject, with grades if relevant.

5 Membership of sports and clubs indicate you are a team player. Hobbies show commitment and a willingness to be challenged. Generic interests should be detailed if possible; e.g. if your hobby is reading, specify your favourite genre or author.

6 Do not include references in the CV, but indicate that they are available.

7 Use bulleted note-form to save space and add impact to statements.

8 Do not try to impress by using a wide range of fonts. A single font, with bold, italics and underlining, used sparingly, will suffice.

9 When outlining your key qualities and skills, back up your statements with evidence to add substance to your claims.

10 Emphasise what you can offer the employer, rather than the other way round. Define your professional goals and relate them to the job in question in one concise sentence.

8 | Numbers

Language focus

Modals in the past

1 Read *The Case of the Dead Landlord* and answer the questions.

1 What was the name of the landlord?
2 What are the names of the three suspects?
3 What possible motive(s) did each suspect have?

It was June, 1953. Inspector Modahl arrived to find a crowd gathered around the victim, whose lifeless body lay on the pavement in front of a ten-storey building.

'His name is Eric Myler,' said a police officer. 'He's the owner of the building. He lives on the top floor and rents out the other flats. They're all one-room studio flats, apparently.'

'Did he fall off the roof?' asked Inspector Modahl.

'No. The door to the roof is locked from the inside and only Mr Myler had the key. His keys were in his pocket when we found him.'

'Any witnesses?'

'Only one elderly lady,' answered the officer. 'Doreen Wallace. She lives on the eighth floor. The poor woman saw the man drop past her front window.'

Inspector Modahl went to see Mrs Wallace in her flat.

'I was changing the light bulb in the lamp above the window when I heard a scream,' claimed Mrs Wallace. 'Then he fell past my window like a sack of potatoes.' Inspector Modahl looked around the flat. It was very small. There was an old bed on the other side of the room, a tiny television standing on a small wooden table, and a small stepladder leaning against the wall. Apart from that, the room was empty.

'What did you do next, Mrs Wallace?'

'Well, I called the police. Then I went down to the street to see if there was anything I could do.'

Inspector Modahl then walked up to the ninth floor and interviewed Micky Trotter, who lived directly above Mrs Wallace.

'I didn't see anything,' said Micky. 'I'm divorced and it was my day to look after the kids, so I've been with them all morning.' Inspector Modahl walked to the window and tried to open it. 'Sorry, Inspector. You can't open that window; I nailed it shut when the kids were born.' Sure enough, the Inspector saw the outline of a nail under the paintwork.

'Did you know the victim very well?' asked the Inspector.

'I'll be honest with you, Inspector,' answered Mr Trotter. 'I hated him. And not just because he was having an affair with my ex. The thing is, he was always after more money. Only last week he told everyone in the building he was going to double the rent. We just can't afford to pay that much each month. I'm not sorry he's dead, to tell you the truth!'

Finally, Inspector Modahl went to the top floor to interview Maggie Myler, the victim's wife.

'I last saw Eric an hour before the accident,' she said. 'He said he had a couple of "jobs" to do, checking the flats in the building, and that he'd be back for lunch. He was probably with that Trotter woman. It's no secret, Inspector – the whole neighbourhood knows about my husband and his affairs.'

'I'm sorry to hear it, Mrs Myler,' said Inspector Modahl, gazing thoughtfully at the beautiful fresh flowers in Maggie's window box.

'Oh, don't worry. The marriage was over anyway. At least I'll have his life insurance money now, though! What do you think happened, though? Any suspects?'

Inspector Modahl turned his head. 'Oh, not just suspects, Mrs Myler. I already know who killed your husband.'

2 Complete the sentences using appropriate forms of the following verbs:

> ~~can't / kill~~   could / fall   could / push
> may / have   might / want   must / change
> ought to / realise   would / damage
> would / increase   wouldn't / be

1 Eric Myler _can't have killed_ himself by jumping off the roof, because the door to the roof was still locked.

2 Maggie Myler _____ to kill her husband because she was jealous of his affairs.

3 Mrs Myler can't have pushed her husband out of the window because her window box _____.

4 Micky Trotter _____ a motive too, because Myler was having an affair with his ex-wife.

5 If Myler hadn't died, he _____ the rent the following month.

6 If his window hadn't been nailed shut, Micky Trotter _____ Myler out of it.

7 Doreen Wallace _____ able to afford the rent if Myler had doubled it.

8 Mrs Wallace wouldn't have been able to change the light bulb on her own, so someone else _____ it for her.

9 Myler _____ out of Mrs Wallace's window while he was changing the light bulb.

10 Mrs Wallace _____ that anyone with their eyes open would have noticed she didn't have a phone.

3 Who does Inspector Modahl suspect, and why?

4 (8.1) Listen to the Inspector and check your answers.

5 Read the dialogues. Match B's replies to the underlying meanings (a–c).

1 A: Look at all this mud on the carpet!
  B: It wasn't me! Ally was playing football outside, so if you ask me it was him.

2 A: So who do you think took the money? Do you think it might have been Denise?
  B: Well, I suppose it's feasible but I just don't think she would do that.

3 A: Has John finished that report yet?
  B: Er, I'm not absolutely sure, but I expect so because he's been writing it all morning.

4 A: Don't say a word! I know what you're thinking! It's terrible. And it cost me nearly £50!
  B: Well, I must say you do look a bit weird. Didn't you know Nicky used to be a hairdresser? She always does my hair.

a) S/he must have done it . _____
b) S/he should have done it. _____
c) S/he could have done it. __2__ , _____

6 (8.2) Listen to the original dialogues and check your answers.

Discourse markers

1 Read about the science of numerology and complete the sentences.

1 Numerology is…   a) modern   b) ancient.
2 Numerology is…   a) simple   b) complex.

Numerology is the study of numbers and the way they reflect personality. The numbers in your birth date and the letters in your name (each letter has a numerical value) reveal a great deal about character, motivation and talents. [1] _____, numerologists can use these numbers to advise on the best time to make investments, get married, change jobs or move house.

Pythagoras, the Greek mathematician who lived from 569–470 BC is said to be the originator of modern numerology, [2] _____ its actual origins go back as far as the Hebrew Kabbalah. In 1911 the science of numerology re-emerged in a book by L. Dow Balliett. [3] _____, in 1931 Florence Campbell published her classic numerology text, *Your Days Are Numbered*. In recent decades interest in numerology has increased enormously, giving it a 'new age' feel. The truth, [4] _____, is that numerology is an ancient art.

[5] _____ it has an ancient heritage, numerology is the easiest to understand of the 'occult arts', which include astrology and alchemy. All you need is your birth date and complete name in order to unlock the secrets that the numbers hold, and no great mathematical calculations are involved. [6] _____, only 11 'core' numbers are used in numerology charts. These are 1–9 and the 'master' numbers, 11 and 22. The numbers, then the individual digits, are added together until the sum is one of the core numbers, each of which represents different characteristics. Then the truth about who you really are is revealed.

2 Which discourse marker is not possible in each case?

1 a) equally   b) yet   c) moreover
2 a) although   b) even though   c) besides
3 a) moreover   b) in addition   c) nevertheless
4 a) whereas   b) though   c) however
5 a) conversely   b) while   c) although
6 a) in fact   b) what's more   c) in contrast

Vocabulary

Expressions with numbers

1 Look at the pictures and match the two parts of the expressions.

1	It's six of one and	a)	square one.
2	It's back to	b)	seventh heaven.
3	First come,	c)	one track mind.
4	They are in	d)	to tango.
5	He has a	e)	first served.
6	It takes two	f)	half a dozen of the other.

2 Match the expressions above with the definitions.

1 to be in the same situation you were in before you started

2 to think of only one thing (usually sex)

3 when two people are both responsible for a bad situation

4 if you arrive before others, you will be attended to first

5 to feel extremely happy

6 used for saying that two things are equally good or bad

3 Complete the gaps with an appropriate expression.

1 That plan fell through again and I'm afraid
_____.

2 Well, it was just as much your fault as mine:
_____, you know.

3 You don't like football; you just like looking at the footballers' legs! You _____, you have!

4 It doesn't matter if you buy it now or next week, _____.

5 I'm sorry I beat you to it, but they did say it was _____.

6 I couldn't believe my luck! I _____ when I heard the news.

4 Complete the sentences with different expressions. The number used is given as a clue.

1 I thought I had made up my mind to take the job, but now I _____. (2nd)

2 As always, I was rushing and I handed in the work _____. (11th)

3 Since I got back from the health farm, I _____. ($1,000,000)

4 I didn't really have a proper sleep, just _____. (40)

5 I wouldn't trust him, he's says one thing and then does another. He's so _____. (2)

6 It's incredible! Since I won first prize, I've just been on _____. (9)

Number prefixes

Many words give an indication of number. Write a word for each definition, using the letters to help.

a) a copy of something, e.g. document: du<u>plicate</u>

b) a ten-year period: deca_____

c) an insect with a hundred legs: centi_____

d) a large crowd: multi_____

e) a single track railway system: mono_____

f) a person who speaks several languages: poly_____

g) a piece of equipment that you use to see distant objects: bi_____

h) a game for one person: sol_____

i) for both men and women: uni_____

j) a unit for measuring computer information: kilo_____

k) a unit for measuring very short periods of time: milli_____

l) a group of four musicians: quar_____

◼ Listening & Vocabulary

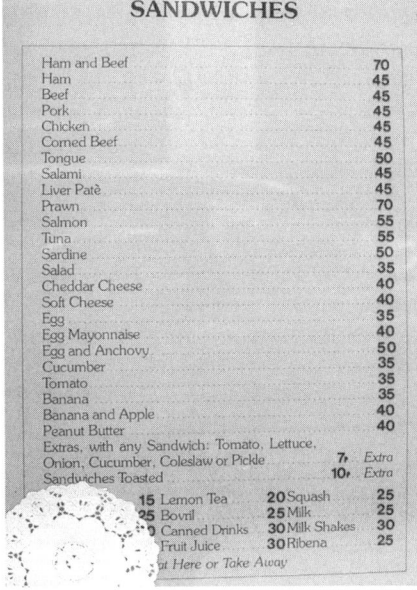

1 **8.3** Listen to six extracts. Write down the numbers that you hear.

1 _____£2.60_____   4 _____

2 _____   5 _____

3 _____   6 _____

2 Listen again. Where are the speakers? What are they talking about?

1 <u>A coffee bar. He's ordering an espresso coffee.</u>

2 _____

3 _____

4 _____

5 _____

6 _____

3 In which sports would you hear these numbers and other references?

1 If it's nil–nil after extra time, we move on to penalties, of course. _____

2 She's had three break points, but now it's back to deuce again. _____

3 That birdie on the last hole has given him the leadership at seven under par with one day's play to go. _____

4 That's an excellent set of scores, look at that! Two 9.7s, one 9.8, two 9.9s and just one 9.4 from the Czech judges. _____

5 The Americans are winning the 100 metres, as they change now from backstroke to front crawl for the final length. _____

6 Over almost 900 games in his career, Anderson averaged 12.4 points and six assists per match. _____

Vocabulary & Reading

A Cross Sum is a type of logic puzzle that is best explained as a a) _mathematical_ transliteration of the crossword. Cross Sums feature regularly in puzzle b) _____ in the United States. In Japan, where the puzzle is called Kakuro, its c) _____ is immense, second only to Sudoku among puzzle publisher Nikoli's famed d) _____. Nikoli named their version *kasan kurosu*, a combination of the Japanese word for 'addition' and the Japanese pronunciation of the English word 'cross'. It then became the catchier e) _____, Kakuro.

Sparked by Sudoku's sensational worldwide success, the Kakuro boom in the West started in September 2005 when *The Guardian* newspaper introduced f) _____ Kakuro puzzles in the UK. The rules are simple, but completing a puzzle takes practice, patience and logical g) _____. Despite the use of numbers and the need, at first, for basic h) _____ and subtraction, it is really a test of logic, not of arithmetic. The aim is to place a i) _____ digit between 1 and 9 in blocks of two to nine empty cells running horizontally and vertically inside a larger grid. The sum of each block should match the target number, or clue, which appears inside shaded cells. No number may be used more than once in each block, so if the target number is 4, and there are two empty cells, the two numbers j) _____ are 1 and 3, not 2 and 2.

Kakuro is slightly more k) _____ than Sudoku, but equally l) _____, and its m) _____ means that the puzzle appeals to all age groups. Once you've learned the rules, which takes seconds, you see signs of n) _____ almost immediately. But it never gets too easy. Addicts say they don't tire of Kakuro because it is so flexible. If completing a 10 by 12 cell grid becomes a piece of cake, it is time to move on to bigger grids, and with Kakuro, size is (almost) everything. It is not like the Rubik's Cube craze in the 1980s, which became a sort of status symbol or sign of extra-ordinary brainpower if you finished it in record time. Kakuro players, it seems, merely report an o) _____ sense of p) _____ as a puzzle approaches completion. And, of course, for the newspapers, such puzzles attract and retain readers. Both broadsheets and tabloids in the UK are reporting increased sales as a result.

---

1 Complete the text using the appropriate form of these words.

a) mathematics	e) abbreviate	i) number	m) simple
b) publish	f) day	j) require	n) improve
c) popular	g) able	k) challenge	o) increase
d) offer	h) add	l) addict	p) satisfy

2 Find words / expressions in the text which mean:

Paragraph **1**

a) enormous _____

b) attracts your attention more _____

Paragraph **2**

c) a major increase in popularity _____

d) basic mathematical calculation _____

e) a pattern of straight lines that cross each other to form squares _____

Paragraph **3**

f) something that suddenly becomes popular _____

g) intelligence _____

h) small format newspaper _____

3 Summary writing. Complete each of these sentences with a suitable answer based on the text.

1 Some people call Kakuro...

2 The name Kakuro...

3 One of the reasons for the game's popularity is...

4 People don't get tired of playing Kakuro because...

5 Unlike the Rubik's Cube craze...

6 It is clear that Kakuro helps to...

4 Complete the puzzle.

1 How do we say these numbers in English?

a) 37 b) 752 c) 5,692 d) 78,016 e) 864,290

f) 7,104,378

2 Complete the rules.

When we say numbers larger than 99 in English, we use _____ after the word *hundred*, except when the number is an exact multiple of 100.

573 _____

700 _____

We also use _____ after the words *thousand*, *million* etc. if the number which follows is less than 100.

4,009 _____

3,000,042 _____

Types of numbers

1 Find the following among the numbers in the box.

1 three prices

2 three fractions with a value less than one

3 four sums

4 a number expressed to two decimal places

5 a percentage

6 a square root

7 a number cubed / to the power of three

8 an odd number

9 an even number

10 a fraction with a value greater than one

11 two ways of writing the time

12 a temperature

4	4 x 3 = 12	$^4/_3$	43%	€43	3 43°
	4 + 3 = 7	$^3/_4$	4 − 3 = 1	√34	$0.34
	4.43	$^1/_3$	4.03pm	43p	$^1/_4$
		4 ÷ 3 = 1.33	03.40	4^3	

2 (8.4) How are the numbers in the box pronounced? Listen and check.

3 Read the texts and match them to the situations.

a) a news report

b) someone giving directions

c) a railway station announcement

d) a political speech

e) a supermarket announcement

① The next train to arrive at platform 7 will be the delayed ¹_____ from Exeter St David's, scheduled to arrive at London Paddington at 15.48. Please note that this train is running slightly later than scheduled, and is now expected to arrive at London Paddington at a) _____.

② Don't miss this week's offers on all frozen foods! Steak and kidney pies down 50p from £2.99 to £2.49. Family-size pizzas down from ²_____ to £1.85. And this week's 'Saver Special' – buy any £1.80 tub of ice-cream and get a second tub for 25% of the normal price! That's two tubs for only b)_____!

③ Financial news now and following the release of yesterday's inflation figures, the markets have opened strongly on the Stock Exchange this morning, with the FTSE 100 share index initially jumping ³_____ points to 5722.62 within the first few minutes of trading, although it has now dropped back slightly to c)_____.

④ The fact is that this government's policies have brought about an economic decline of such magnitude that inflation is now running at ⁴_____, compared with a high of only 2.5% during our last government, and there are already nearly d)_____ more unemployed than when this government came to power, the total having risen to over 800,000.

⑤ As you come into the town, go through the lights and then after three-quarters of a mile turn left onto Brookvale Avenue. About ⁵_____ metres further on you'll pass a pub on the right, and, after another 400 metres or so, take the road off to your left. Keep going for another e)_____ miles and you'll see the house on the right, just before the church.

4 Put the numbers in gaps 1–5 in the texts.

a) 200

b) 13.25

c) 84.16

d) £3.49

e) 3.9%

5 (8.5) Listen to the complete texts and write the rest of the missing numbers in gaps a–e.

9 | Space

▍Language focus

Giving information about things

1 Read the clues describing a TV programme. How many clues do you need to read before guessing the programme?

1 <u>Addictive to watch</u>, it originally appeared on Dutch TV in September 1999, since then <u>its format</u> has been cloned in 32 other countries.

2 At least one former participant has been treated <u>in a psychiatric hospital</u>, and another has tried to commit suicide.

3 The internet is a vital element of <u>the show's success</u>, <u>providing</u> continuous, 24-hour coverage via <u>video cameras</u>.

4 It has occasionally been accused of being <u>pseudo-pornographic</u>, although the most popular versions have been more like <u>live soap operas</u>.

5 Other criticisms include accusations of voyeurism and exploitation of gullible, vulnerable members of the public by TV companies <u>eager to make</u> a quick profit.

6 Participants live in a <u>specially-designed</u> house, permanently <u>within view of video cameras</u>, and with <u>no media contact </u>with the outside world.

7 Participants are set tasks, <u>communicated</u> to them by an anonymous individual who issues instructions, <u>which are designed to test their teamwork abilities and community spirit</u>.

8 To obtain more cash for provisions, participants may gamble <u>some of their weekly allowance</u> on the successful completion of tasks, although their income is reduced if they fail.

9 Participants have access to a '<u>diary room</u>', where they can express their thoughts and frustrations about other participants.

10 Each week, participants nominate fellow housemates <u>whom they would like to see removed from the house. The people with the most nominations</u> are named and the public vote to decide who is evicted.

2 Find two examples of the following from among the underlined items in the sentences.

a) compound adjectives _pseudo-pornographic_ _____

b) noun modifiers (noun + noun) _____ _____

c) possessive structures _____ _____

d) quantity expressions _____ _____

e) prepositional phrases _____ _____

f) adjective + infinitive structures _____ _____

g) present or past participles as the subjects of clauses _____ _____

h) noun phrases _____ _____

i) relative clauses _____ _____

3 (9.1) Listen to three people talking and answer the questions.

Who...

1 doesn't like Big Brother? _____

2 has changed their original opinion about the show? _____

3 thinks it reveals a lot about the idea of being famous? _____

4 understands why people like it? _____

5 thinks everyone has extreme opinions about it? _____

6 finds the show addictive? _____

4 Listen again and complete the extracts.

Speaker 1

1 It's _____, but then who cares if no one really understands why it's so popular?

2 ...after a while you realise that they're just being natural, kind of forgetting they're _____.

3 Like a _____ version of that Jim Carrey film, *The Truman Show*.

Speaker 2

4 ...which was won by the only contestant _____...

5 As long as _____ guessed the truth she'd be allowed to stay in the house.

6 _____ her win it I thought, well, if that doesn't say it all about the idea of reality TV and the concept of celebrity, I don't know what does.

Speaker 3

7 Well, it's _____, if you ask me.

8 There are _____ who are cultured, intelligent people...

9 I'd rather go and sit in the park to see it rather than sit glued to the _____ hour after hour.

5 Add each word or expression to one of the categories in Exercise 2.

Inversion after negative expressions

1 Read the e-mail and answer the questions.

1 What is the purpose of the e-mail?

2 What do you think the relationship between Gerald and Mary might be?

```
┌─────────────────────────────────────────┐
│ ▣▣          E-mail              ▣▣     │
├─────────────────────────────────────────┤
│  📄    🖨    📤    📎    📧   ▶   ✖   📇 │
│ File  Print  Send  Attach Reply Forward Cancel Address │
├─────────────────────────────────────────┤
│ Hi Mary,                            ▲   │
│ I've been thinking about this sports    │
│ centre thing, and I reckon it's worth   │
│ writing to complain to the              │
│ council. The whole idea has been put    │
│ together in a really half-baked way,    │
│ and I can see it turning out to be a     │
│ nightmare for this part of the town.    │
│ Nobody asked us what we thought, and    │
│ I think it'll just make the existing    │
│ problems worse. More places to go just  │
│ encourages more kids to get             │
│ involved, meaning more trouble for us   │
│ unless we get more police patrolling    │
│ the area, and I can't see that          │
│ happening. They've got enough on their  │
│ plate! I can just imagine it – the      │
│ minute it opens there'll be kids        │
│ swarming all over the place with        │
│ their beer cans and ghetto blasters.    │
│ Anyway, we can't let it go ahead as it  │
│ stands. The least they should do is     │
│ send someone round to ask us            │
│ what we think; I might take what they   │
│ say a bit more seriously then. What do  │
│ you think? Shall I put something in     │
│ writing?                                 │
│ Gerald                               ▼  │
└─────────────────────────────────────────┘
```

2 Complete Gerald's letter to the council with the words in the box. Use the information in the e-mail.

> at no   little does   no sooner   ~~not only~~
> on no occasion   only   only then   should

10, Seaview Road
Harrington
HTZ 7BL

Dear Head Planning Officer,

I am writing to express my concern about the proposals for a new sports and social club in the harbour area. [1] Not only is this an example of appalling town planning, but the implications for the surrounding area are potentially disastrous.

My first criticism of the project is the lack of consideration shown to local residents. [2]_____ point did the council or the construction company think to consult our opinions when the plans were being drawn up. Secondly, the council has publicly stated its wish for the new centre to be a meeting place for young people in order to limit the numbers of youths who gather late at night in other areas of the town. [3]_____ the council realise that rather than reducing the problem in other areas its proposal is likely to simply extend it to this area as well. [4]_____ with a considerable police presence will such groups be prevented from causing a disturbance and the police are surely busy enough as it is. Consequently, [5]_____ will the centre open than people will start using the surrounding area as a convenient place to stand around drinking and playing music. [6]_____, as far as I am aware, have groups of youths congregating in public areas done anything other than make life a misery for those who live nearby.

Under no circumstances [7]_____ this proposal be approved in its present form. Along with other local residents, I expect, at the very least, a visit from a local planning officer who will listen to and act upon our concerns. [8]_____ will we be prepared to consider seriously the supposed benefits that this project may conceivably have in the future.

Yours faithfully,

Gerald Morris

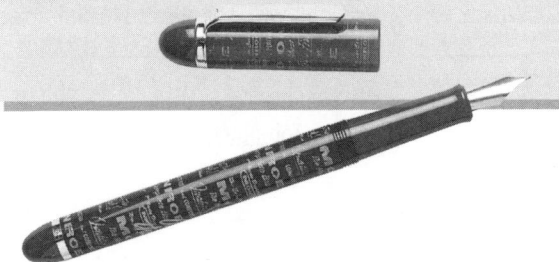

Vocabulary

Expressions with *space*

adj + *space*	phrases
enclosed space	space of time
parking space	~~to look/stare into space~~
advertising space	(to be) spaced out
breathing space	a waste of space
outer space	space-age

I just need some space!

Complete the gaps with an appropriate expression from the box.

1 I think she was in a state of shock; all she did was ____stare into space____ for hours.

2 …and suddenly he turned up out of the blue, like from _____ or something.

3 Newspapers make a lot of money from selling _____.

4 I need to get out! I can't bear being in an _____ for such a long time.

5 Those tablets make you feel a bit _____ for a while. That's perfectly normal.

6 You've done a wonderful job in an incredibly short _____.

7 You could spend half an hour trying to find a _____ at this time of day.

8 We'll give you some _____, and then perhaps you'll be ready to make a decision.

9 I don't know why you carry on seeing him; he always was _____.

10 That new building looks totally _____; the design is ultra-modern.

Listening

1 **(9.2)** Listen to six short conversations. Match the dialogues (1–6) and the places (a–f).

Dialogue 1   a) flat
Dialogue 2   b) art gallery
Dialogue 3   c) pub
Dialogue 4   d) bank
Dialogue 5   e) computer shop
Dialogue 6   f) school

2 Listen again to answer questions A and B in the table.

a What kind of space are the people talking about in each dialogue?

b Which verb combines with the word *space* in each case?

Speaker	Kind of space	Verb + space
1	on a computer hard drive	leave enough space
2		
3		
4		
5		
6		

Saying 'I don't know': *Try the interactive activity for this topic on your CD-ROM.*

Urban areas

1 Complete the gaps with words from the box.

> gentrified area   ghettos   shanty town   squats   suburbs   townships

1 Rocinha in Rio de Janeiro is the biggest _____ in the world. They call it a *favela*.

2 This part of town was really downmarket before it became a more _____. Now the house prices are soaring.

3 Soweto and other places in South Africa were called _____ and were originally designed to house the black population.

4 I think it's only fair that some empty flats become _____, although I know it's illegal.

5 During the Second World War, Jewish people were forced to live in _____ in Poland and Germany.

6 There's no point living in the _____ in this city; it takes so long to get to the centre of town.

2 Which of the words have a negative connotation?

ZOOM IN: *over*

1 Find two examples of *over* in the text on page 58. Match them with uses 1–4.

1 preposition (followed by a noun / a number)
The plane flew over our heads.

3 adverb (meaning more or above)
There are over 150,000 habitants in Rocinha.

over

2 all over + the place, the floor, the world, etc.

4 prefix (used with verbs = too much)
I overslept this morning.

2 Look at the expressions with *over*. Match each one (a–h) with a meaning (1–8).

a) Over the last five years we've seen a big increase in violence.
b) He spilt his drink all over the floor, the silly thing!
c) There's a lot of time left over, if you want to ask questions.
d) Can you move over a bit? I haven't got enough room.
e) There is a lot of speculation over his future as president.
f) Over and above their basic salaries, lots of city workers enjoy huge bonuses.
g) I've told you over and over not to do that!
h) They said the film would be over by seven.

1 remaining
2 in addition to
3 during
4 finished
5 towards the side
6 everywhere
7 repeatedly
8 concerning

3 Complete the sentences with *over-* + verb.

Verbs frequently used with *over-* include: *book, charge, cook, do, dose, eat, estimate, rate, simplify, spend, use and work*. These verbs are often used adjectivally or as a passive form. They overcharged me. or I was overcharged.

1 I'm sorry I'm so late today, I've got no excuse this time, I just _____.

2 I'm afraid the plane is _____; you'll have to spend the night in Rome.

3 Be careful not to _____ the rice; it will stick to the pan.

4 It's easy to _____ in a foreign country, because you're not familiar with the currency.

5 We are all _____ and underpaid. It's always the same story!

6 That argument is just _____ things. It's actually much more complicated than that.

Vocabulary extension

People and spaces

Match each person (a–j) to the space (1–10) they might occupy.

a) a tramp
b) a teacher
c) a rich city dweller
d) a dentist
e) a soldier
f) a skier
g) a holidaying couple
h) a market trader
i) a photographer
j) a gardener

1 a chalet
2 a hovel
3 a shed
4 a darkroom
5 a staffroom
6 a stall
7 a barracks
8 a surgery
9 a villa
10 a penthouse

Reading

1 What kind of buildings are in the photo? Read the text to find out.

City of Dreams

There is no space left in Macau, the Portuguese colony which returned to Chinese rule in 1999. With figures of more than 17,000 people per square kilometre, Macau has the highest population density in the world. So, like its neighbour Hong Kong, a mere 60 kilometres away, the authorities are looking to the sea to reclaim land.

The Macau government's latest plan is the City of Dreams; a huge project which will include an underwater casino with capacity for 450 gambling tables and 3,000 slot machines. The $1 billion scheme will also house deluxe serviced apartment blocks, 2,000 hotel rooms, a shopping mall and a 4,000-seat performance hall. The scale of the project is huge, covering over 465,000 square metres of floor space.

The resort will be located on Macau's Cotai strip, entirely made up of reclaimed land, which developers hope to fashion as Macau's answer to the Las Vegas Strip. The new complex is expected to open in mid-2009. With this venture, Macau is predicted to overtake Las Vegas as the world's biggest gambling market, with the territory's casinos projected to bring in more than $5 billion in gambling revenue as newly-affluent mainland Chinese flood to Macau. The reason for Macau's success? It remains the only place in China where gambling is legal.

2 Are the statements about the text true (T) or false (F)? If false, explain why.

1 Macau is no longer a Portuguese colony. ____
2 Hong Kong's authorities also build on the sea because of lack of space. ____
3 Macau already has the biggest gambling market in the world. ____
4 The people coming to gamble in Macau are the established Chinese upper class. ____
5 Macau is the only place in China where you can gamble. ____

3 Find words in the text to match the definitions.

1 to contain   _____
2 luxury   _____
3 to design with skill   _____
4 a business plan   _____
5 income from business activities   _____
6 to move in large numbers   _____

A disastrous trip: Try the interactive activity for this topic on your CD-ROM.

Guided writing: *A proposal*

1 Choose the best definition of a proposal:

a) A summary of various options and alternatives from which the reader is invited to make a final choice.

b) An outline and justification of a course of action, recommended as a means of achieving a stated aim.

c) A description of a problematic situation, highlighting how the situation came about and the risks.

2 Read the proposal and suggest an appropriate title.

TITLE

Introduction
The aim is to develop the site to ensure maximum benefit to the town whilst minimising potential negative consequences for the surrounding area.

Development plan
The site will be dominated by a sports centre which will boast all-weather pitches, an indoor swimming pool and sports hall, a state-of-the-art gym and a sauna/steam room. Fitness classes will be offered for all ages and abilities. An adjoining youth club will provide games machines, pool tables and vending machines offering a wide range of snacks and non-alcoholic drinks. It will be open every evening from 5–9pm, and will be free to all 15- to 18-year-olds.

Potential benefits
Current leisure facilities are inadequate, and a sports centre will help rectify this situation: the site being conveniently located near the town centre. The result will be a stronger sense of community and a fitter population. The youth club will help cater for the needs of young people by providing premises for the 15–18 age group to gather socially in an area otherwise lacking in sufficiently spacious and suitably-equipped alternatives.

Management of potential problems
Research revealed concerns that young people congregating in the area will disturb local residents, and that under-age drinking may occur. To guarantee this is not the case, two adult volunteers will supervise the club during opening hours. Anyone acting in an antisocial way or breaking club rules will be banned, and repeat offenders will be reported to the police.

Conclusion
A sports centre and youth club will undoubtedly benefit the town and its residents, providing much-needed facilities with minimum associated risk.

---

3 The following are essential components of a successful proposal. Underline examples in the text.

a) a relevant, neutral title

b) separate sections and sub-headings

c) clearly specified rationale behind the proposal

d) formal register

e) a detached, impersonal style, e.g. using the passive to add 'distance'

f) a tone suggesting conviction rather than vagueness and uncertainty

g) a positive ending, emphasising how your proposal will achieve the desired outcome

4 Successful proposals require language which is persuasive without being over-emotional. Find words or expressions in the proposal to match the definitions (1–10).

1 have something impressive and worthy of pride (*vb*) ____boast____

2 very modern and up-to-date (*adj*) _____

3 large selection or variety (*n*) _____

4 correct, put right (*vb*) _____

5 ideally situated (*adj*) _____

6 fulfil the requirements of (*vb*) _____

7 with the necessary facilities and installations (*adj*) _____

8 to make certain (*vb*) _____

9 without any doubt (*adv*) _____

10 urgently required (*adj*) _____

5 An area of your town is to be redeveloped. As Chair of the local Residents' Committee you are to submit a proposal to the Town Council, including an outline of your committee's recommendations and any potential benefits and drawbacks. Write your proposal using the guidelines given here.

10 The end

Language focus

All / every / each

1 Read the following quotations and correct the underlined word or phrase if necessary.

1 It is better to keep your mouth closed and let people think you are a fool than to open it and remove <u>all of</u> doubt. *(Mark Twain, American novelist)* ____all____

2 Life is a foreign language; <u>all</u> men mispronounce it. *(Christopher Morley, American novelist)* _____

3 <u>Every of</u> great dream begins with a dreamer. Always remember, you have within you the strength, the patience, and the passion to reach for the stars to change the world. *(Harriet Tubman, US activist)*

_____

4 One of the most important things one can do in life is to brutally question <u>all single</u> thing you are taught. *(Bryant H. McGill, American poet)* _____

5 If you obey all of the rules, you miss <u>each of</u> the fun. *(Katherine Hepburn, American actress)* _____

6 I try to live what I consider a 'poetic existence'. That means I take responsibility for the air I breathe and the space I take up. I try to be immediate, to be totally present for <u>all</u> my work. *(Maya Angelou, US poet)*

_____

7 <u>All</u> the world's a stage and most of us are desperately unrehearsed. *(Sean O'Casey, Irish playwright)* _____

8 Women marry men hoping they will change. Men marry women hoping they will not. So <u>every</u> is inevitably disappointed. *(Albert Einstein, German scientist)* _____

2 Complete these quotations using the phrases in the box.

a) **each of / both of** my other senses	e) resign yourself to the influences **of each / each of**
b) **every / each** of which makes us bigger	f) **Every / All** day is the world made new.
c) **each / all** moment of life is a miracle and mystery	g) In **each of / each** us there is a private hope and dream.
d) the welfare of **all / all of**	h) **every / all** human problem

1 Live each season as it passes; breathe the air, drink the drink, taste the fruit, and ____. *(Henry David Thoreau, American novelist and philosopher)*

2 We must not allow the clock and the calendar to blind us to the fact that _____. *(H.G. Wells, British novelist)*

3 Every morning is a fresh beginning. _____. Today is a new day. Today is my world made new. I have lived all my life up to this moment, to come to this day. *(Dan Custer, American writer)*

4 Life is a series of experiences, _____, even though it is hard to realise this. *(Henry Ford, American industrialist)*

5 I was afraid that by observing objects with my eyes and trying to comprehend them with _____, I might blind my soul altogether. *(Socrates, Greek philosopher)*

6 There is always a well-known solution to _____ – neat, plausible, and wrong. *(H. L. Mencken, American journalist)*

7 The welfare of each is bound up in _____. *(Helen Keller, American writer and activist)*

8 _____ which, fulfilled, can be translated into benefit for everyone and greater strength for our nation. *(John F. Kennedy, Former US president)*.

3 Circle the correct words in Exercise 2 (a–h).

| Albert Einstein | Katherine Hepburn | Helen Keller | H. G. Wells |

Participle clauses

1 Match the names (1–8) with extracts (a–h).

1 Paris Hilton __a__

2 Fernando Alonso _____

3 Peter Jackson _____

4 Ang Lee _____

5 Bridget Jones _____

6 Keira Knightley _____

7 *The Da Vinci Code* _____

8 The 'Tour de France' _____

a) (raise) _____ in the luxurious surroundings of Beverly Hills, she has become a classic example of someone who is 'famous for being famous' and is in many ways the archetypal modern celebrity, rarely off the front pages of the gossip magazines.

b) (make) _____ his name in his native New Zealand, where he directed several independent cult films, he reached a much wider audience with the blockbusting *The Lord of the Rings* trilogy and a spectacular, big-budget remake of *King Kong*.

c) (regard) _____ as the most gruelling individual race in the world, it often passes through parts of Spain and England as well as the country with which it is most closely associated, before finishing on Paris's *Champs-Elysees*.

d) (earn) _____ the title of 'Sexiest Movie Star of All Time' later the same year, this English actress was the third youngest nominee for the Best Actress Oscar for her performance in an adaptation of Jane Austen's *Pride and Prejudice* in 2005.

e) (create) _____ by Helen Fielding as the writer of a fictional diary, this accident-prone young woman has become something of a heroine for single women around the world, with her constant struggle to balance the demands of work, friends and lovers.

f) (win) _____ a Best Foreign Film Oscar in 2000 for *Crouching Tiger, Hidden Dragon,* this Taiwan-born director repeated his success and won the Best Director award in 2006 for his controversial romance *Brokeback Mountain*.

g) (capture) _____ the imagination of more and more conspiracy theorists each year, this thriller tells the story of American academic Robert Langdon and his attempts to solve both a violent murder and the 2000-year-old mystery of the Holy Grail.

h) This Spaniard became Formula One's youngest World Champion when he finished third in the 2005 Brazilian Grand Prix, breaking the record previously held by Emerson Fittipaldi, (end) _____ five years of dominance by Michael Schumacher in the process.

2 Complete the participle clauses by putting the verbs in brackets in the correct form.

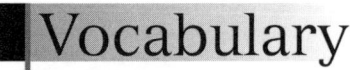

Vocabulary

Euphemisms

1 Look at these sentences and underline the expressions related to death. What does the euphemism mean in each case?

1 At my age, you know, you do think about <u>passing away</u>... *dying*

2 Our loved ones are usually wrapped in a white shroud. _____

3 Living with loss is something that you just get used to. _____

4 I'm not ready to kick the bucket yet! _____

5 I think we're going to have our dog put down. It's cruel to keep him alive. _____

6 Many religious people believe that the deceased go to a better place. _____

7 To confirm the burial arrangements you'll need to talk to our grief therapist. _____

8 Our soldiers were given instructions to terminate with extreme prejudice. _____

9 What was your relationship with the dearly departed? _____

10 All our clients receive a dignified burial. _____

2 Are the expressions formal (F), neutral (N) or informal (I)? Use a dictionary to help you decide.

3 Many euphemisms belong to categories (a–d). Classify the examples. What do the euphemisms mean?

a) Acronyms (*TLC* – tender loving care)

b) Circumlocution (using alternative words to avoid directness: *to be under the influence* – to be drunk)

c) Doublespeak (describing actions in neutral terms: *collateral damage* – unintended military damage)

d) Political correctness (*visually impaired* – blind)

1 There are increasing numbers of **asylum seekers** in our country. <u>refugees – (c)</u>

2 The doctor won't say it, but I think we're talking about **the big C** here. _____

3 I'm just going **to powder my nose**, I won't be a moment. _____

4 There are a lot of **sex workers** in that area. _____

5 Are you going to tell him **the news** or shall I? _____

6 There were a number of **casualties** in the **intervention**. _____

7 **Senior citizens** have the same rights as all of us. _____

8 So where do you stand, are you **pro-life** or **pro-choice**? _____

9 I've never seen an **adult movie**. _____

4 The following expressions are examples of doublespeak.

a Match them with their more neutral or negative translations (a–h).

1 freedom fighter	a) unemployed person
2 to outsource	b) guerrilla / terrorist
3 customer service representative	c) alternative lifestyle
4 to downsize	d) to kill
5 to neutralise a target	e) to fire staff due to business restructuring
6 taxpayer	f) to hire cheaper staff elsewhere
7 jobseeker	g) bank clerk
8 counter culture	h) citizen

b Are these terms corporate / military / social?

1 _____ freedom fighter – military _____

2 _____

3 _____

4 _____

5 _____

6 _____

7 _____

8 _____

🌐 ***Sleep idioms:*** *Try the interactive activity for this topic on your CD-ROM.*

5 Complete the gaps with the appropriate expressions from Exercise 4.

1 If you have any further queries, our _____ will be delighted to be of assistance.

2 Reports have come in that US forces have _____ an important _____ in the early hours of Friday morning.

3 The classes are designed for _____ and the elderly – those who have got some time on their hands.

4 We've _____ that department to Indian staff, because it will be more economical.

5 It depends on your point of view, but I would call them _____, because I believed in their cause.

6 The policy will not be popular with most _____, who will see their monthly income reduced again by further increases.

7 The company has _____ over the past few years as part of a long-term cost-cutting strategy.

8 The main _____ of the sixties was the hippie movement.

Film language

Match the film language (1–10) with the definitions (a–j).

1 special effects   a) a photograph of somebody / something taken from a very close position
2 fade-out   b) a fight using guns
3 tear-jerker   c) a sad film or story that makes you cry
4 long-shot   d) an exciting end in which it is not clear what will happen next
5 slow motion   e) film action that is shown more slowly than real speed
6 close-up   f) a shot in a film which gradually disappears
7 cliffhanger   g) a view of a scene that is shot from a considerable distance, showing a broad perspective
8 shoot-out   h) unusual sound / image in a film, created artificially using various technical methods
9 screenplay   i) music played during a film
10 soundtrack   j) story someone writes for a film

Film genres

Match the famous film title (1–10) with its genre (a–j).

1 *Murder on the Orient Express*   a) costume drama
2 *Psycho*   b) biopic
3 *Emmanuelle*   c) western
4 *The Living Dead*   d) spoof
5 *Paris, Texas*   e) disaster
6 *Sense & Sensibility*   f) horror
7 *Gandhi*   g) blue / adult
8 *Brokeback Mountain*   h) whodunnit
9 *Airplane*   i) thriller
10 *Titanic*   j) road movie

1 Look at the four illustrations. Who feels awkward in each situation?

2 🔊10.1 Listen to four dialogues.

1 Match the situations to the drawings (a–d).
2 Why is the moment 'awkward'?
3 What is the wrong thing to say in each case?
4 What do you think the person should have said?

3 🔊10.2 Listen to four new dialogues. Circle the expressions that you hear.

1 It's / It'd be a pleasure.
2 What is / on earth's the matter?
3 ...in case you didn't hear / hadn't heard.
4 Please accept / expect my condolences.
5 Please be / do our guest.
6 I can't / can appreciate that.

4 In what awkward situation might you use these expressions?

1 I was so sorry to hear of your loss.
2 Oh, you shouldn't have!
3 It's really delicious, I'm just so full now.
4 I'm terrible with names, honestly.
5 I have a memory like a sieve.
6 I can assure you that it won't happen again.

How to ... say goodbye

The language we use when saying goodbye in English depends on whether we are communicating in writing or verbally.

1 Which of the following would normally *only* be used to say goodbye in writing?

All the best	Cheerio	Look after yourself	Ta-ta
Best regards	Cheers	See ya	With love
Best wishes	Have a good one	Take care	Yours faithfully

The language we use to end a letter or an e-mail depends on the context and the nature of the relationship we have with the person or people we are addressing.

2 Are these statements true (T) or false (F)?

a) 'Kind regards' is too colloquial for formal e-mails. Use 'Yours' instead.
b) If you start your letter with 'Dear Dr Wallis', an appropriate ending would be 'Yours faithfully'.
c) 'Kisses' is a typical way to end a letter or e-mail to a close friend of the opposite sex.
d) 'Best wishes' is a suitable way to end an informal letter to an acquaintance, but would be too impersonal for a close friend or family member, and too personal for a business letter.
e) Avoid using -ing forms at the end of business letters (e.g. 'I am looking forward...'), as it can sound informal and colloquial.

3 Read these extracts and check your answers to Exercise 2.

1
Anyway, that's all my news. How about you? I haven't heard anything from you for a while. Let me know how thing's are going if you get a chance.
Love,
Katie xxx

2
I am available at short notice should you wish to discuss my proposal in person. I look forward to hearing from you at your earliest convenience.
Yours
Tony Huang

3
Dear Dr Wallis,
Thank you very much for your kind invitation, which my wife and I are delighted to accept. We therefore look forward to meeting you on July 13th.
Yours sincerely
Michael Pirroni

4
It would also be very helpful if you could include a list of hotels which you personally recommend, as I am not very familiar with the area.
Kind regards
Melanie Kanegawa

5
Anyway, Jim has told us a lot about you and it will be wonderful to meet you at long last. Please let us know what time your flight is due to arrive and we will be happy to meet you at the airport.
Best wishes
Maggie and Hal

4 Which one of the endings is not an appropriate alternative for the texts?

1 a) All my love b) In love c) Lots of love

2 a) Expecting to hear from you b) Looking forward to hearing from you c) Awaiting your reply

3 a) Yours Faithfully b) Yours c) Sincerely

4 a) Regards b) Best regards c) High regards

5 a) With best wishes b) Warm regards c) Happy wishes

5 Put the lines of each dialogue in the correct order.

1
a) Ta-ta.
b) Anyway, I won't keep you because you must have loads of things to organise.
c) Right-o. Have a lovely time. And send us a postcard!
d) Will do. Speak to you in a couple of weeks. Ta-ta.
e) OK. Well, I'll send you a text when we get there – it'll be cheaper than phoning.

2
a) Well, I'd best be off, otherwise I'll miss my train.
b) Thanks, Jo. Take care.
c) OK, I'll e-mail it to you tomorrow. Look after yourself.
d) So, thanks again for the meal. You must let me know the recipe.
e) Yes, it's the last one as well.

3
a) OK. Cheerio then.
b) So that's a table for four for 9.30 on Saturday.
c) Oh yes, of course. So, we'll see you on Saturday then.
d) That's right. Oh, and non-smoking if possible.
e) No problem at all. We're actually non-smoking throughout.

4
a) Yeah, let's do that. I could do with a night out. I'll give you a ring.
b) Right, I must dash. I'm late for work. Good to see you, anyway.
c) Cool. Cheers, then.
d) Yeah, we should arrange to go out sometime for a few beers.
e) Cheers, mate. Have a good one.

6 🎧 10.3 Listen and check your answers. Who do you think is speaking in each case, and in what context?

7 Find examples of the following from the underlined expressions in the dialogues.

1 three excuses for leaving

2 an expression suggesting a desire for someone to enjoy themselves

3 two expressions expressing concern for someone's health and safety

4 two expressions referring to the next time the people will meet or speak to each other

5 three informal or colloquial expressions meaning 'Goodbye'

Reading

(20 marks)

1 Complete the article using the phrases below. One of them is not used. (_____ / 5)

a) and so he was well-placed to design Roboraptor

b) It is absolutely worth it, of course

c) it is hard not to keep thinking about the price tag

d) now one of the most popular toys in the world

e) it will spontaneously begin to explore its environment

f) children were getting less and less interested in toys

At some point in the past ten years the British toy industry began to notice something troubling: ¹_____. They wanted mobile phones and PlayStations instead. In the USA, where the phenomenon has gone the furthest, it is known by the clunky acronym *kagoy* – Kids Are Getting Older Younger. To invent a new toy in this climate, you need a peculiar combination of adult commercial savvy and insight into the child brain. Thanks to *kagoy*, you really need a toy that isn't a toy: something that can slip through the defences of resistant children while preferably also appealing to grown-ups too.

Mark Tilden is a former NASA scientist, ²_____. 'Robotics is usually too serious,' Tilden says today in his company's showroom, in a Hong Kong office complex called Energy Plaza. 'I wanted to make a robot that can kick, walk and to do any disgusting things you want, yet still be cute. In the 1960s, we were promised that we would one day have flying cars, honeymoons in orbit and robots in our homes. I can't do much about A and B, but I can do C,' Tilden says. NASA 'used to give me a million

dollars to build one robot to crash on Mars. Instead, I now make toys for a million children in the hope that they will play with them by themselves.' He came to China in 2002, he is fond of saying, 'to work for Santa... This is the only place in the world where you can build this kind of stuff so that it can be sold for just $120.'

$120 is not that cheap for a toy, and during the first few seconds of an initial encounter with Roboraptor ³_____. But then you figure out how to put Roboraptor into 'guard mode' (in which it will lash out at people) and into 'playful' mode (in which it will wiggle its tail if you touch it). You discover that if you leave it unattended for three minutes, ⁴_____, trundling across the floor until it hits a wall. When Roboraptor behaves 'intelligently' you catch yourself feeling impressed and, when it doesn't, you catch yourself responding as you would to a clumsy toddler, rather than as you ought to respond to 132 plastic parts, 235 metal ones and 191 electrical components. But Roboraptor is not, primarily, intended to be cute. 'This is the first robot that really has the ability to scare children,' Tilden

says proudly. 'Our previous robots could annoy your cat. Roboraptor can hunt him.'

Roboraptor was officially launched in Britain in June. Choosing a launch date so long before Christmas enabled everyone involved to test the water. The launch was followed by a public-relations assault involving interviews with Tilden in various gadget-oriented lads' mags, plus children's TV advertising. By next Sunday evening, Tilden's invention will doubtless have been the subject of much attention in living rooms across Britain. First, though, anyone who receives a Roboraptor will have to figure out how to get it opened. Because of Roboraptor's sensitive moving parts, it must be attached to its thick cardboard base by four screws and numerous plastic bindings. It takes a long hunt for the right size of conventional screwdriver before I finally get it out of the pack. ⁵_____. But it is not hard to envisage the whole unpacking procedure being the cause of a few family arguments, or last-minute screwdriver hunts, this Christmas Day.

Batteries, needless to say, are not included.

2 Decide if the following sentences are true (T) or false (F). (_____ / 5)

1 The British toy industry is more interested in making toys for adults than for children. T / F

2 Mark Tilden chose to work in China because he could buy a lot of cheap toys there. T / F

3 The writer thinks Roboraptor is too expensive. T / F

4 Families with pets are advised against buying Roboraptor. T / F

5 Roboraptor was heavily promoted in Britain in the period before Christmas. T / F

3 Complete the sentences by choosing the correct discourse marker. (_____ / 5)

1 To be a successful toy inventor nowadays, it is important to be commercially aware. **Conversely / What's more**, an understanding of how children's brains work is also necessary.

2 On the whole, the visions of the future which people had in the 1960s were inaccurate, **although / besides** Mark Tilden feels he in a position to make one of them a reality.

3 Roboraptor can be programmed to react to people if they touch it. **Similarly / Even though**, it will start moving spontaneously if it is ignored after a few minutes.

4 Roboraptor is only a machine. **While / Nevertheless**, there are times when you react to it in the same way you would react to a child.

5 It is quite difficult to get the Roboraptor out of its box. **However / Moreover**, it's worth it when you do!

4 Complete each sentence with an appropriate participle clause. Use the verb in brackets. (_____ / 5)

1 _____ more interested in 'adult' products, children have gradually lost interest in toys traditionally aimed at their age group. (become)

2 _____ for NASA, Mark Tilden is suitably experienced for designing toys like Roboraptor. (work)

3 _____ the only place where hi-tech products can be made very cheaply, China was an attractive destination for Tilden. (be)

4 _____ with Roboraptor for the first time, it takes a while before you fully appreciate what it can do. (play)

5 _____ carefully in its box because of its delicate components, Roboraptor might provoke arguments if people can't find the right screwdriver they need to open it. (pack)

Listing

(20 marks)

1 ◀TY.2▶ Listen to five people talking about the idea of happiness and match them with the situations. (_____ / 5)

a) relaxing at home   b) meditating   c) making money   d) playing sport   e) reflecting on the day

2 Decide if the sentences are true (T) or false (F). (_____ / 5)

1 Daryl always finds it very easy to control his emotions. T / F

2 If Andres were offered a million pounds he would refuse it. T / F

3 Julia admits *Friends* isn't very intellectually challenging. T / F

4 Trevor feels particularly happy when he completes enjoyable tasks. T / F

5 For Michelle, the most important thing about playing tennis is doing a winning shot. T / F

3 Choose the correct alternative in each case. (_____ / 5))

1 Daryl knows how to meditate because he **used to / would** be interested in Buddhism.

2 People **are always insisting / use to insist** that money can't buy happiness, but they'll always accept money if you offer it to them!

3 Julia **is ever / is forever** watching old episodes of *Friends*, even when she knows exactly what's going to happen.

4 When she was asked what made her happy, Margaret Thatcher **would / will** say 'a ticked-off list'.

5 From time to time Michelle **is hitting / will hit** a fantastic shot which makes her feel like the world's best player.

4 Correct the mistakes in the following sentences. (_____ / 5)

1 Daryl is able to make himself happy all time he is in a stressful situation.

2 According to Andres, if you offered a million pounds to a group of people, all them would accept it.

3 Julia has seen each episodes of *Friends* at least six times.

4 Trevor feels happy at night when he thinks of every of the things he's managed to do that day.

5 Michelle plays lots of games of tennis and usually hits at least one great shot in each of.

Writing

(15 marks)

You have been asked to contribute to a guidebook about the area where you live. Write an entry for the guidebook about either:

a) your home town or another town you know well; or **b)** a building in your town.

Language Passport

Self-assessment grid

- *Use this checklist to identify what you **can do** after completion of the three preceding units, as well as to identify your own language-learning **priorities.***
- *Use the right-hand column as a reference to where you can find **more help.***

<table>
<tr><td colspan="3"></td><td>I can do this</td><td>This is a priority</td><td>For more help</td></tr>
<tr><td rowspan="8">Understanding</td><td rowspan="3">Listening 🎧</td><td>I can follow extended speech even when it is not clearly structured and when relationships are not signalled explicitly.</td><td>☐</td><td>☐</td><td>Unit 6, SB, pp. 57, 58, & 61.
Unit 7, SB, pp. 66 & 71.
Unit 8, SB, pp. 73, 75 & 78.
Unit 9, SB, pp. 82, 85, & 87.
Unit 10, SB, pp. 91, 92, & 94.
Flashback 2, SB, p. 101.</td></tr>
<tr><td>I can understand a wide range of idiomatic expressions and colloquialisms, appreciating shifts in style and register.</td><td>☐</td><td>☐</td><td>Unit 6, SB, pp. 55 & 61.
Unit 8, SB, p. 73.
World English 4, SB, pp. 80–81.
Unit 9, SB, pp. 82 & 87–88.
Unit 10, SB, pp. 92, 94, & 96.
Flashback 2, SB, p. 100.</td></tr>
<tr><td>I can understand lectures, talks and reports in my field even when they are linguistically and propositionally complex.</td><td>☐</td><td>☐</td><td>Unit 8, SB, p. 77.
Unit 9, SB, p. 88.
Unit 10, SB, p. 91.
Flashback 2, SB, p. 102.</td></tr>
<tr><td rowspan="4">Reading 📖</td><td>I can read complex reports, analyses and commentaries where opinions, viewpoints and connections are discussed.</td><td>☐</td><td>☐</td><td>Unit 6, SB, p. 59.
Unit 8, SB, pp. 72–73.
Unit 9, SB, p. 86.
Unit 10, SB, p. 97.
Flashback 2, SB, p. 100</td></tr>
<tr><td>I can summarise orally.</td><td>☐</td><td>☐</td><td>Unit 6, SB, p. 56.
Unit 7, SB, p. 65.
Unit 9, SB, p. 84.</td></tr>
<tr><td>I can read contemporary literary texts (an extract from a novel) with ease.</td><td>☐</td><td>☐</td><td>Unit 7, SB, p. 67.</td></tr>
<tr><td>I can go beyond the concrete plot of a narrative and grasp implicit meanings, ideas and connections.</td><td></td><td></td><td>Unit 8, SB, p. 74.
Unit 9, SB, p. 89.
Unit 10, SB, pp. 92–3.</td></tr>
<tr><td>I can recognise the social, political or historical background of a literary work.</td><td>☐</td><td>☐</td><td>Unit 6, SB, p. 60
Unit 7, SB, p. 67.</td></tr>
<tr><td rowspan="4">Speaking</td><td rowspan="2">Spoken Interaction 👄↔👄</td><td>I can use language flexibly and effectively for social purposes, including emotional, allusive and joking usage.</td><td>☐</td><td>☐</td><td>Unit 7, SB, pp. 65 & 70.
Unit 10, SB, pp. 91 & 94.
Takeaway English, WB, p. 64.</td></tr>
<tr><td>I can express my ideas and opinions clearly and precisely, and can present and respond to complex lines of reasoning convincingly.</td><td>☐</td><td>☐</td><td>Unit 6, SB, p. 58.
Unit 7, SB, p. 69.
Unit 9, SB, p. 89</td></tr>
<tr><td rowspan="2">Spoken Production 👄</td><td>I can give an extended description or detailed account of something, integrating themes, developing particular points and concluding appropriately.</td><td>☐</td><td>☐</td><td>Unit 6, SB, p. 61.
Unit 9, SB, pp. 85.</td></tr>
<tr><td>I can orally summarise texts.</td><td>☐</td><td>☐</td><td>Unit 6, SB, p. 56.
Unit 7, SB, p. 65.</td></tr>
<tr><td rowspan="2">Writing</td><td rowspan="2">Writing ✒</td><td>I can write texts which show a high degree of grammatical correctness and vary my vocabulary and style according to the addressee, the kind of text and the topic.</td><td>☐</td><td>☐</td><td>Unit 8, SB, p. 77
Unit 9, SB, p. 83
Unit 10, SB, pp. 93 & 95.
Communication Activities, SB, p. 117.</td></tr>
<tr><td>I can present a complex topic in a clear and well structured way, highlighting the most important points, for example in a composition or report.</td><td>☐</td><td>☐</td><td>Unit 7, SB, p. 67.
Unit 9, SB, pp. 83 & 89.
Guided Writing, WB, p. 59.
Communication Activities, SB, p. 124.</td></tr>
</table>

Unit 1 | Attitude

Language focus

Continuous verb forms

1   1T   2C   3C   4T   5C   6T

2   1 are seeing the new Harry Potter film later   2 I have seen
3 had been seeing   4 I had seen him before   5 saw the boys
shoplifting   6 have been seeing   7 were seeing each other
for coffee this afternoon   8 see Dan

Perfect verb forms

1   1i   2j   3f   4c   5b   6g   7h   8d   9a   10e

2   unfinished: 3, 8   recent: 1, 5, 6, 10
finished at a definite time: 2, 4, 7, 9

Continuous & perfect verb forms

1   1 is becoming   2 you've broken   3 was approaching
4 are creating   5 passed   6 has been moving

2   1 spoken – a news report, 2 spoken – a doctor talking to
a patient, 3 written – a police incident report, 4 spoken –
a football commentary, 5 written – a text message, 6 spoken –
a weather forecast

Spoken stance markers

1   Speaker 1: allowing pubs to stay open 24 hours a day
Speaker 2: banning mobile phones in schools
Speaker 3: removing speed limits on some roads
Speaker 4: banning smoking at work

1: I've got mixed feelings about it, to be honest. I can see
why lots of people object to the idea, because there's
enough trouble caused by rowdy behaviour after closing
time already, but if you ask those in favour they'd say that's
exactly the point. The trouble is the result of everyone
pouring out on to the streets at the same time. If licensing
laws were a bit more flexible, people would be able to pace
themselves a bit more rather than feel they had to get as
much down them as possible before last orders. And
presumably everyone would go home at different times so
you wouldn't get as many gangs of drunks roaming the
streets looking for trouble after half eleven. All in all I
reckon it's worth a try.

2: There's no real evidence that they're bad for your health
in any way, is there? Some people think they affect our
brains, especially when we're young. I can't see it myself.
So kids can use them to cheat in exams? Students have
been cheating in exams since exams were invented, for
goodness sake! And they can be distracting if kids forget
to turn them off? Well, it doesn't take much for the teacher
to remind them at the start of the lesson. Basically, there
are some adults who seem to enjoy spoiling kids' fun just
for the sake of it, and inevitably they're the ones trying to
introduce this ban. Personally, I think anything which helps
children communicate should be encouraged. I think it's a
terrible idea.

3: To me it makes perfect sense. Let's face it, there'll always
be people who break the law because frankly there'll
always be people who are prepared to run the risk of
picking up a fine, causing a pile-up or even getting
themselves killed. That's just their attitude to life! The
government might not be too keen on the idea because
they'd lose a fair amount of revenue from speeding fines,
but that'd be offset by the fact that it costs a lot to enforce
speed restrictions in the first place. Undoubtedly there
would be some lunatics who would let the new freedom

go to their heads, but the novelty would soon wear off.
Anyway, I'm sure I read somewhere that most crashes
occur when people are doing less than 40 kilometres per
hour, so if anything it might even have a positive effect.

4: Apparently they've already done this in parts of America,
and also in Ireland I think. I can understand it when it
comes to restaurants and other indoor public places, but
these are places which people go to by choice, to some
extent, whereas when it comes to the office, well, many
people spend a third of their lives there, and hardly
because they choose to! Where would we draw the line?
Would people be searched by their boss when they arrived
at work, in case they might be trying to sneak a packet in
so they can disappear off to the toilet for a quick puff every
20 minutes? Admittedly it's not good for anyone's health,
so perhaps there should be some restrictions, but
a complete ban? That's a bit over the top, I'd say.

2   1 presumably   2 All in all   3 Basically   4 inevitably   5 frankly
6 Undoubtedly   7 Apparently   8 Admittedly

Vocabulary

Multiple meanings: lift

1   1 withdraw / repeal   2 driven / taken   3 plagiarism
4 shoplifting / stealing   5 assisted / helped   6 feel happier
7 improve

2   1 match   2 drag   3 lead   4 match   5 fit   6 firm   7 firm   8 fit
9 lead   10 drag

Informal meanings of attitude

1 negative feelings and inappropriate behaviour
2 a proud way of behaving that is usually seen as rude
3 weird, original and eye-catching

Describing attitudes

1   1 positive   2 new   3 ambivalent   4 changing   5 favourable
6 hostile

2a   1 very determined, not willing to change your opinion
2 relaxed   3 not caring about the seriousness of a situation
or other people's views   4 very politically correct or
fashionable

2b   **Negative:** laid-back, cavalier, right-on.
Positive: uncompromising

Reading & Vocabulary

1 faith   2 creator   3 prophets   4 praying   5 worship   6 preach
7 fasting   8 pilgrimage

Listening

1   Buddhism 144,453 Christianity 37,338,486 Hinduism 552,421
Islam 1,546,626 Judaism 259,927 Sikhism 329,358

2   1 Islam 2 Buddhism 3 Judaism

1: Well, I'll tell you a little about my religion. There are
about one and a half million of us living in the UK and it
seems that the population is growing. I'm sure you know
that we worship in a mosque. Well, sometimes it's called
a masjid. Now, outside every mosque, or well … just inside
the entrance, there's a place where worshippers can
remove and leave their shoes. Inside, there are no pictures

or statues, because there can be no image of Allah, who is purely spirit. Then, there's a niche in one of the walls, called a mihrab, this shows the direction that the worshippers should look in order to face Mecca, of course. Most mosques have a minaret, that's a tall thin tower. A muezzin stands at the top of the tower and calls us to prayer five times a day. The thing is not all mosques in the UK have a minaret, although the main ones do, like the most important mosque in London, in Regent's Park. P: Well, that's all for now, tomorrow we'll…

2: There are about a hundred and fifty thousand of us living in the UK. One difference between our religion and others is we can worship either at home or at a temple. It's not essential to go to a temple and worship with others. At home, we set aside a room as a kind of shrine, there will be a statue of Buddha there, candles, and an incense burner. The best known of our temples are in China and Japan and these are designed to symbolise the four elements: Fire, Air, Earth, and Water. Obviously, all temples contain an image or a statue of Buddha. You can sit on the floor barefoot facing an image of Buddha and chant. You can listen to monks chanting from religious texts, perhaps accompanied by instruments, and you can take part in prayers. There are many forms of worship; the main thing is what you feel inside. Well, our religion became especially popular in the UK in the sixties and what differentiates it from groups in other countries is that there's really no such thing as institutionalised prayer here, the groups we have are mainly concerned with the practice of meditation, rather than chanting or bowing…

3: Well, as I was saying, there must be just over a quarter of a million of us living in the UK at the moment but unfortunately that figure seems to be dropping fast. Our most important day is the Sabbath, our holy day, and those who are observant keep its laws and customs from sunset on Friday until sunset on Saturday. We believe that there's a single God who not only created the universe, but with whom every one of us can have an individual and personal relationship. This is a covenant relationship, in exchange for the many good deeds that God has done and continues to do for our People. Community is very important for us and there are many different types of movements within our faith. Well, I belong to the liberal movement, this is very different from orthodox communities – for one thing in its attitude to women – in our community, women can lead services and become rabbis. We were also the first Jewish movement to allow girls to go through the Bat-Mitzvah ceremony, which is equivalent to the traditional male Bar-Mitzvah which is held at the age of 13…

3 a3 b1 c3 d1 e2 f2 g2

Zoom In

1 a) no such thing b) for one thing

…what differentiates it from groups in other countries is that there's really no such thing as institutionalised prayer…
…this is very different from orthodox communities – for one thing in its attitude to women…

2 a) for one thing b) no such thing

3 1 (not) a thing 2 the latest thing 3 just one of those things 4 there's no such thing 5 the thing with him 6 for one thing 7 no bad thing 8 just the thing

The Real Thing: well

1 1c 2d 3a 4b

1 Well, I'll tell you a little about my religion.
2 …I'm sure you know that we worship in a mosque. Well, sometimes it's called a *masjid*.
3 Well, as I was saying, there must be just over a quarter of a million of us living in the UK at the moment…
4 Well, that's all for now, tomorrow we'll…

2 1 Well, that's not quite true. 2 Well, go on, spit it out!
3 Well, we'll just have to wait and see.

1
A: Just give it up! C'mon you never liked the job in the first place.
B: Well, that's not quite true.
2
A: Listen, I've got something to tell you.
B: Yeah?
A: It's hard to put into words.
B: Well, go on, spit it out!
3
A: So, did you have a word with him, then?
B: Yeah, I told him I wanted more money.
A: And what did he say?
B: He said, 'Well, we'll have to just wait and see, won't we?'

3 1 to express your doubt about what someone has said
2 to indicate that you are waiting for someone to speak
3 to indicate uncertainty (about increasing B's salary)

4 Student's own answer.

Guided writing

1 Neighbours causing noise pollution by playing loud music at night.

2 To request advice and suggestions from other readers; anxious not to cause offence.

3 Indirect questions; passive forms.

4 Student's own answers.

5 Speak to the local environmental health department; take private legal action.

6 Young people disturbing local residents by riding their motorcycles up and down the street.

7 Scaring the youths away by buying an aggressive dog; threatening the youths with a gun; playing loud opera music to persuade them to move elsewhere.

8 B 1 to give sensible, professional advice 2 serious and professional 3 factual language; passive forms 4 student's own answers
C 1 to express frustration; to indicate that the first writer's problem is less serious than her own 2 desperate 3 descriptive language 4 student's own answers
D 1 to be humorous and dismissive 2 sarcastic 3 descriptive language 4 student's own answers
E 1 to suggest a radical and exaggerated solution to the problem of noisy youths 2 bossy and arrogant 3 ellipsis 4 student's own answers
F 1 to be humorous by pointing out that one solution would be to do something which creates yet another problem 2 sarcastic and amused; exasperated 3 indirect question; excessively formal language 4 student's own answers

9 Student's own answers.

10 Student's own answers.

Language focus

The future with will

_1_ a2 b7 c1 d4 e6 f3 g5 h8

_2_ 1 will be doing 2 will have been repairing 3 will start
4 will have been flying 5 will be performing 6 will be
having 7 will have gone 8 will be

_3_ 1 will have finished the exam, 2 will be preparing to close
the shop, 3 will be reopened / will have been reopened,
4 will be waiting for her luggage, 5 will have been playing
for two hours, 6 will have been raining for several hours,
7 will start, 8 will be OK to eat

Cohesive devices

_1_ a4 b– c6 d– e– f2 g3 h1 i5 j–

_2_ 1 in the beginning 2 at first 3 such as 4 as a result of
5 as well as 6 otherwise

_3_ a) d b) b c) j d) e

_4_ a) therefore b) after that c) otherwise d) thus

Vocabulary

New communication words

_1_ 1 PDA 2 texting 3 wi-fi 4 broadband 5 emoticons

_2_ **both:** emoticon, PDA
internet: blog, domain, chat rooms, wi-fi, broadband, spam
mobile phones: texting, ring tone, hands-free, SIM card

_3_ 1 broadband 2 a domain 3 emoticons 4 texting 5 SIM card
6 PDA 7 hands-free 8 ring tone 9 chat rooms 10 wi-fi
11 spam 12 blog

The Real Thing: all

_1_ a)

_2_ 1 for all I know 2 by all means 3 by all accounts 4 all in all
5 all being well 6 for all 7 in all 8 all along

1
A: Is it very valuable … your car?
B: Not sure. For all I know, it's worth a fortune.

2
A: Do you mind if I wait here?
B: By all means.

3
A: Of course, he's still a bachelor.
B: Well, by all accounts he was married once, you know,
   a long time ago now.

4
A: Well, she's gone now.
B: I know, it's sad to see her go, but all in all it's for the best.

5
A: Well, see you again some time…
B: Yes, all being well, next summer…

6
A: I've come to like the city. Haven't you?
B: Yes, for all its faults, you can't help but like Mexico City,
   there's just something about it…

7
A: So, let's book a table, shall we?
B: OK, how many of us are there in all?

8
A: That holiday was just too cheap, wasn't it?
B: Yes, I knew all along there was something suspicious
   about it.

_3_ for all I know – to say something might be true
by all means – to give permission
by all accounts – according to what people say
all in all – to sum up
all being well – hopefully
for all – despite
in all – in total
all along – the whole time

_4_ Student's own answers.

Vocabulary extension

Clothes idioms

_1_ a) suit b) socks c) knickers d) belt e) cap f) trousers
g) collar h) cuff i) gloves j) sleeve

_2_ 1 sleeve 2 belts 3 collar 4 trousers 5 socks 6 belt 7 glove
8 knickers 9 suit 10 cuff 11 cap 12 collar

_3_ 1h 2k 3c 4j 5l 6b 7g 8a 9e 10d 11f 12i

Takeaway English

_1_ (Sample answer) very stilted, not enough involvement with
public, dry and not very animated.

Text messaging has grown in popularity very rapidly.
By mid-2004 texts were being sent at a rate of 500 billion
messages per annum. At an average cost of ten US cents
per message, this generates revenues in excess of 50 billion
dollars for mobile telephone operators and represents close
to a hundred text messages for every person in the world
per year. There are clear reasons for its popularity. Text
messages or SMS are quick and easy to send – it takes a
matter of seconds – and it is much cheaper to text than
make a call.

Text messaging might seem just innocent fun but its use
has serious and negative implications for society. Students
can cheat in exams by texting answers to each other.
Political rallies have been organised via SMS chain letters,
electoral campaigning as well – like the Spanish elections
in 2003 held soon after the Madrid terrorist attack – and
even presidents have been forced to resign. In Malaysia,
you can divorce your partner by text messaging. In
Australia, race riots were said to have been incited by SMS.
And yet there are positive aspects to messaging. In
emergencies, texting has certainly saved lives, most
famously in cases such as Hurricane Katrina…

_2_ (Sample answer) make tone friendlier, use more questions /
cohesive devices.

_3_ More rapport established, use of question tags / we, all,
our / cohesive devices.

You see, text messaging has grown in popularity very
rapidly. I'm sure most of us here have sent a text message
to somebody today, haven't we? Now, as a matter of fact,
by mid-2004 texts were being sent at a rate of 500 billion
messages per annum. And we all know what that means,
don't we? At an average cost of ten cents per message, all
this generates revenues in excess of $50 billion for mobile
telephone operators and represents close to a hundred text

messages for every person in the world per year. Clearly, then, there are good reasons for its popularity. Text messages or SMS are quick and easy to send, after all it takes a matter of seconds and then it's much cheaper to text than make a call, isn't it?

Text messaging might seem just innocent fun but its use can also actually have serious and negative implications for society. Well, students can cheat in exams by texting answers to each other. Political rallies have been organised via SMS chain letters, electoral campaigning as well – we should recall here the Spanish elections in 2003 held soon after the Madrid terrorist attack – and even presidents have been forced to resign. In Malaysia, as strange as it may seem, you can divorce your partner by text messaging. In Australia, race riots were said to have been incited by SMS. And yet there are positive aspects to messaging, aren't there? In emergencies, texting has certainly saved lives, most famously in cases such as Hurricane Katrina. Haven't we all had to turn to our mobile phone for help, at some time or another...?

4 (Sample answers) 1 I'm sure most of us here have sent a text message to somebody today, haven't we? And we all know what that means, don't we? ...it's much cheaper to text than make a call, isn't it? 2 Haven't we all had to turn to our mobile phone for help, at some time or another? 3 And we all know what that means, don't we? ...we should recall here...; Haven't we all had to turn to our... 4 as strange as it may seem; we should recall here...

5 (Sample answers) a Mobile phone use should be banned in some pubic spaces, shouldn't it? / don't you think? b Don't people / you think that mobile phones are bad for your health? c All of us have a mobile phone these days. d In some countries, such as Hong Kong which I visited recently, mobile phone use is common even in places like the cinema.

6 1c 2d 3e 4b 5a

How to ...

1 1b 2a 3c 4c 5a 6b 7c 8d 9b 10d

2 1e 2b 3a 4c 5f 6i 7j 8d 9g 10h

3 a) that kind of thing b) give or take c) more or less d) I'm not sure that's strictly true e) somewhere in the region of f) or words to that effect g) umpteen h) just gone i) whatsisname j) roughly speaking

5 a **Softening the message:** I'm not sure that's strictly true
b **Approximating / Paraphrasing:** give or take, more or less, somewhere in the region of, or words to that effect, just gone, roughly speaking
c **Generalising:** that kind of thing
d **Replacing words:** umpteen, whatsisname.

6 Student's own answers.

Unit 3 | Hate

Language focus

Adding emphasis

1–3 Student's own answers.

4&5 1 we did go – c, 2 what it also meant was that – f, 3 absolutely dreadful – a, 4 surely you've flown often enough – b, 5 the point is this was supposed to be – d, 6 The thing is, once he's sitting down – d, 7 a building site was what the hotel was – e, 8 it wasn't at all like – b, 9 the only time it did work – c, 10 The beach was utterly filthy – a, 11 All we did all week was wander round the shops or sit in bars watching English football on the TV – f, 12 Fifteen, I wrote! – e

🔊 3.1

A: Hi Trish, how was your holiday?
B: Oh, don't ask!
A: Oh no! Why? What happened? You didn't go in the end?
B: No, we did go, but honestly, Rosa, everything went wrong. First the taxi to the airport broke down, so we thought we'd missed the flight. Then, when we got there, we found out the flight was delayed by five hours.
A: That was lucky!
B: Well, yes, I suppose it was, but what it also meant was that we had to spend the first day of our holiday sitting in a departure lounge ... and you know how Felix hates flying! So he was getting more and more nervous...
A: I bet he was!
B: Anyway, the flight itself was about the worst I'd ever been on. Absolutely dreadful. Lots of turbulence so we had to keep our seatbelts on all the time. And the food was even worse than usual; can you imagine?
A: Yeah but surely you've flown often enough to know what airline food is like.
B: I know, but the point is this was supposed to be one of the best airlines. What a joke! The kids were off colour for the next few days, and I'm sure it was what they'd eaten on the plane.
A: How did Felix get on in the end?
B: Oh he was fine! The thing is, once he's sitting down on the plane he's OK. He fell asleep before we took off and slept pretty much all the way!
A: At least something went right, then?
B: Yes, but then we got to the hotel and found it was next to a building site. In fact, a building site was what the hotel was! It wasn't at all like the picture in the brochure. The swimming pool was only half built, the balcony we'd been promised wasn't safe, the lift was out of order nearly the whole time. The only time it did work it got stuck halfway up and we had to wait for a mechanic to come and get us out! Unbelievable!
A: What about the resort? What was that like?
B: It was better than the hotel, but not by much! The beach was utterly filthy, covered with cigarette ends and empty beer cans, and the sea wasn't safe to go in most days. All we did all week was wander round the shops or sit in bars watching English football on the TV. Felix and the kids didn't mind that too much, but it's not really my cup of tea as you know.
A: Well, no!
B: Let's just say I ended up writing three times more postcards than usual. Fifteen, I wrote! I sent you two, by the way. Have you got them yet?
A: No, but they take ages to...

6 1 she is so 2 I do know 3 you simply double-click 4 when I did finally get it going 5 He actually threatened to call the police 6 It was totally unreal

Uses of get

1 1c 2a 3b 4d 5f 6e

2 a) 1c, b) 3b, c) 5f, d) 6e, e) 2a, f) 4d

3 1 people thinking 2 to know someone 3 themselves made 4 her to drink 5 older 6 stabbed

4 1b 2c 3e 4f 5a 6d

Vocabulary

Expressing annoyance

1 1 formal 2 neutral 3 neutral 4 informal 5 neutral 6 informal

2 (Sample answers) 1 This whole situation is really bugging me. 2 That's so irritating. He's always late. 3 Smoking in restaurants really pisses me off. 4 It really annoys me that we never have enough money. 5 This is so bothersome, how many times do I need to tell you? 6 That really irritates me, so don't do it again!

3 1) It drives me up the wall 2) It drives me crazy 3) It drives me round the bend 4) It gets my goat 5) It gets under my skin 6) It gets on my nerves

4 (Sample answers) 1 It drives me absolutely / really / quite / totally up the wall 2 It really gets on my nerves

Vocabulary extension

bother

1 1 sorry to bother you 2 don't bother 3 can't be bothered 4 I'm not bothered 5 the bother 6 keeps bothering

1 Oh, sorry to bother you but would you mind closing the window?
2 A: Listen, I'll give you a hand with that, it's heavy.
   B: Oh, no, please don't bother; I can manage fine, thanks.
3 A: So, what are you up to tonight?
   B: Well, there's a party, but I'm so tired, I can't be bothered to go.
4 I'm not bothered whether we go on holiday or not! We'll have a good time whatever we do!
5 I didn't want the bother of going to the shops, so I bought it on the internet.
6 If he keeps bothering you, you should call the police.

2 a5 b1 c2 d6 e4 f3

3 1 infinitive / to, 2 gerund / –, 3 gerund / with, 4 – / about

(3.3)

1 It was very late, so I didn't bother to phone back.
2 That's OK. Don't bother giving me the present now, wait till my birthday.
3 Why bother with renting a flat, if you can buy one so cheaply?
4 It's not worth bothering about, the money's lost and that's that!

4 (Sample answers)
1 don't bother yourself – don't worry because it will be too much inconvenience for you.
2 oh, don't bother – it's not necessary, I'm better off without your help or gifts.

(3.4)

1
A: Look, you can't stand up throughout the whole coffee break. Let me find you a chair.
B: Oh, please, don't bother yourself; I'm fine, honestly I am!

2
A: I'll make it up to you, I'm sorry love…
B: Oh, don't bother. I've had enough. I don't want anymore of your stupid presents!

Word-building

1 1 appearance 2 concentration 3 enjoyment 4 fellowship 5 purity

2 1 beautiful 2 friendly 3 likeable 4 natural 5 responsive 6 scandalous

3 ambitious, anxiety, committed, considerate, generosity, loyalty, passionate, respectful, sensitivity, willing

Reading

1 perceptions 2 individuality 3 intimacy 4 leadership 5 boredom 6 appearance 7 sincerity 8 mysterious 9 beneficial 10 spontaneity

Listening

1 a3 b4 c1 d5 e2

1: Well, it's very simple really, when they win I love them with all my heart but when they lose, well I'm just all over the place. I get really angry and I hate them for it, I really do. The good thing is that at the moment, they're on a winning streak, so I guess you could say that right now, it's a love–love relationship. I know, it's terrible for your happiness to depend on this but I'm not the only one! There are lots of other mad people like me around.

2: I'm not from round here, so it doesn't matter how long you've been somewhere, you tend to feel like this is no place for me. I guess it's normal. Anyway, I often think I made the best decision in the world coming here, I love the place, but then if someone's rude to me, if I have a bad experience somewhere, it can ruin everything. In general, the people here are OK, but they can be really nasty when they want. You don't want to get on the wrong side of them, that's for sure.

3: You know when he's behaving himself, I love him to bits, but you know it's awful when he plays up in public, you know they do that a lot when they've got an audience, getting excited and barking like mad and, of course, that's very demanding – it can all be a bit embarrassing really. He gets all the attention and I feel a bit out of place. Anyway, I should just relax about this; I know it's not normal to feel upstaged by a puppy!

4: I suppose my love–hate relationship is the most obvious one in the world! But I guess when it's a member of your family, it's different anyway, it must be quite common to love someone one minute and hate them the next. Anyway, what really gets me about my mother-in-law is when she criticises and has no right to. I hate it when she starts off saying something like 'I know it's not my place to criticise,' then you know you're going to be in for it.

5: Well, once you get on the right side of her, it's OK. That's always the way, I reckon and I managed to do that in my first week. I don't know what it is, but I've made quite a few mistakes recently and well she doesn't say anything about it, but I know she doesn't approve, cos she won't talk to me for days afterwards and I hate her for that, so I start to ignore her too. It's crazy but I guess I know my place. That's why I say it's a love–hate relationship really.

Because, after a while everything's forgotten and I can go into her office and have a nice chat about anything. Weird, isn't it?

I can't help thinking I'm the only one who feels like this.

2 1 Speaker 3, 2 Speaker 5, 3 Speaker 1, 4 Speaker 2, 5 Speaker 4

3 Speakers 1, 2, 4 feel that their type of love / hate relationship is shared by others. Speakers 3, 5 feel that theirs is unusual.

▮ Zoom In

1 1 all over 2 it's not my 3 out of 4 know my 5 no (place) for

🎧 **3.6**

1 …but when they lose, well I'm just all over the place.
2 …she starts off saying something like, 'I know it's not my place to criticise…'
3 He gets all the attention and I feel a bit out of place.
4 It's crazy but I guess I know my place.
5 …you tend to feel like this is no place for me.

2 1 To be all over the place: to be upset
2 It's not my place to: to say / do something that is not appropriate for you or is not your responsibility
3 Out of place: inappropriate or uncomfortable
4 To know one's place: to know your role / position (e.g. in an organisation)
5 No place for: not an appropriate setting for
Examples 2, 3 and 5 have similar meanings.

3 1 going places 2 fell into place 3 lost my place 4 neither the time nor the place 5 as if you owned the place

4 (Sample answers) good, best, safe, right, wrong, nice, busy, quiet, strange, public, meeting, hiding, market, etc.

▮ Guided writing

1a (Sample answers) a) a personal website, a series of postings with time and date b) like a normal website c) different subjects, e.g. sport, current affairs d) from cyberspace e) you just need a name and an internet address

1b URL: internet address; commentary: review of other websites; posting: a paragraph with a title, date and time; profile: biography / personal details

2 🎧 **3.7**

A: I keep reading about things called blogs and wonder if, like me, our listeners have any questions about blogs? Well, in the studio today is Rachel Jackson who is going to tell us what exactly a blog is. Welcome to the programme Rachel.
B: Hi Tom and thanks for having me on the show. I hope I can tell you all you want to know about blogs! Basically, a blog is an on-going, personal website, with an internet address, which you may also see called a URL. Blog writers, who often call themselves bloggers, write about things they are interested in and post their thoughts on the internet for anyone to read, along with links to other websites and perhaps a commentary which explains why these websites are worth visiting.
A: That sounds interesting; I'd like to have a look at one.
B: Well, the fact is if you spend any time at all surfing the web these days you'll have definitely come across blogs, or weblogs, to give them their full name, already. There are millions of them, in all shapes and sizes. The thing is you might not have known they were blogs!
A: So how will I know a blog when I see one?
B: At first glance a blog looks very much like a website.

Basically, though, a blog consists of a series of paragraphs – the postings – each with a title and with the date and time underneath. There may also be a link next to each posting, which allows you to add your own comments and read the comments of others. The most recent postings appear at the top, so you can easily read what's new. Down the side of the page you will probably see links to recommended websites and archives of previous postings. Many blogs also include a profile of the author. And every blog needs a name, of course!
A: And are there blogs dedicated to different topics? You know, if I want to read about, say, current affairs or sport?
B: Well there is something for everybody out there! Finding it can be difficult though but … there are things called blog directories. These are virtual filing systems which search the internet for blogs and try to categorise them. An internet search will turn up lots of blog directories, choose one and click on it. Inside you will normally find files for different subjects, and if you open one you'll find a list of blogs. Take your pick!
A: So where did blogs come from? How did they start?
B: They just emerged out of cyberspace! Blogs started to appear in the late nineties and gained in popularity after 2000. The early ones were mostly lists of recommended links. Since then, they've evolved into something different. Now anyone who fancies being a writer – even the most technically-challenged of us – can easily become a blogger!
A: Sounds like fun. Where do I start?
B: It's really easy, even if you know next to nothing about computers! Have a look at my blog and follow the 6-step plan!

3 1 You will get access to more features, such as adding photos or sending texts to your blog. 2 Appearance, colour scheme, layout. 3 Because people have been sacked for criticising their boss on their blog. 4 Because opinions can be spread by linking between different blogs. 5 Send the address to friends, include it on your website and include it on postings you make on other blogs; update your blog frequently, be patient.

4 Student's own answer.

5 Student's own answer.

6 Student's own answer.

Unit 4 | Relationships

Language focus

Model verbs of obligation, necessity & prohibition

1 a4 b6 c1 d7 e3 f2 g5 h8

2 1 can't 2 need 3 mustn't 4 have to 5 should 6 can
7 shouldn't 8 don't have to

Model verbs of deduction & possibility

1 1 in New York, in 1979, 2 nine, 3 nine, 4 not at all

2 a) can't b) must c) must d) must e) could f) can g) could
h) can't i) must

3 2

4&5

S: So, where do we start?
A: Well, look for the row or column with most numbers already filled in, this one here, column 8. There are two numbers missing: 5 and 6 see?
S: OK, but how do we know which goes where?
A: Easy. We know that D9 is a 5. Now, because each number appears only once in a row, the 5 here tells us that D8 can't be a 5.
S: Aha! So it must be the 6?
A: Exactly! And the 5 must go in G8. There, our first complete column!
S: Oh, I see. It's easier than it looks, then. Let me do the next one on my own. This one here, E7. Right, this box already has a 1, 3, 5, 7 and now a 6, and row E has a 9 and a 4 as well, so E7 must be an 8, right?
A: Ah, but what about a 2? We don't have one of those yet.
S: Oh. No, we don't. So E7 could be an 8 or a 2?
A: Well, no. Look carefully. Look at the last column, there's an 8 in it, right?
S: OK. So?
A: So, neither E9 nor F9 can be an 8.
S: Oh, I see what you mean. But there's no 8 in this column, column 7. So, E7 or F7 could both be an 8. That doesn't really help us.
A: Wrong again! Look at this row here, row F, what's the first number in the row?
S: 8.
A: So?
S: So … ah, so F7 can't be an 8. I see! And E7 must be an 8. Am I right?

6 1 can't; must 2 could; might 3 can't; must 4 can't; might
5 can't; might

7

	1	2	3	4	5	6	7	8	9
A	6	8	5	2	3	7	4	9	1
B	9	1	3	4	5	8	6	2	7
C	7	2	4	6	9	1	5	8	3
D	4	3	9	1	8	2	7	6	5
E	1	6	7	9	4	5	8	3	2
F	8	5	2	7	6	3	9	1	4
G	2	4	6	3	7	9	1	5	8
H	3	7	8	5	1	6	2	4	9
I	5	9	1	8	2	4	3	7	6

Model verbs of ability

1 doesn't manage to 2 can be able to 3 managed to 4 could
5 could pass 6 could

Vocabulary

Phrasal verbs: Relationships

1 (Sample answer) d, g, a, c, h, b, e, f

2 1 chat him up 2 they got on well 3 asked Sophie out to the cinema 4 had fallen for each other 5 go out together 6 move in / settle down (together) 7 put up with 8 fell out 9 to break up

Vocabulary extension

1 **positive:** be into, have a crush on, have a soft spot for, hit it off with, think the world of
negative: have it in for, be hung up on, two-time, walk out on, dump.

2 **positive:** 1 have a soft spot 2 hit it off 3 have a crush 4 are into each other 5 think the world of her
negative: 6 two-timing 7 hung up on 8 dump 9 has it in for me 10 walked out on

Easily-confused words

1 They are false friends in many Latin-based languages.

2 1 partner 2 a date 3 sympathetic 4 arguing 5 present 6 remember 7 commitment 8 intend

3 a) couple: two people, often married
b) appointment: an arrangement to meet (formal)
c) kind: considerate, generous
d) discussing: talking about something
e) actual: existing in fact, real
f) remind: cause someone to remember
g) compromise: an agreement made by making concessions
h) pretend: simulate

Takeaway English

1 Conversation 1: One person's car is blocking another person's drive and car. / The former was visiting somebody in the area and it took longer than expected.

Conversation 2: Girl is upset because she is waiting for her friend who has not shown up. / The boy believed that they were meeting at nine, and not at eight.

Conversation 3: Girl did not appear at a party the night before and didn't ring to explain. / She says that she was tired and didn't have the right mobile number to phone.

(4.2)

1
A: Oh, thank goodness, finally!
B: What?
A: Well, can't you see that your car's blocking my drive?
B: No, I didn't see … I was just…
A: What do you mean you didn't see?
B: I mean, I wasn't aware…
A: Eh?
B: Er … The thing is … I was going to drop this off for a friend, I was only going to be a second, but in the end, well … he wasn't in … and, well, you see … it all took a lot longer than I expected, I mean, I didn't do it on purpose…
A: Erm … Well, I think you should show a bit more consideration in the future … I mean, really … I haven't got all day…
B: I'm terribly sorry, I should've … oh, I just didn't realise, OK?

2
A: Hi, Mark!
B: Ah… Hi!
A: Where are you?
B: What?
A: Where are you, for heaven's sake?
B: What do you mean?
A: Er, hello!... We were meant to be meeting tonight, at eight?
B: Oh no! Was it eight? Are you sure?
A: Of course I'm sure!
B: Aah … sorry about that! It's just that, I've got us written down for nine, here…
A: Well, it wasn't nine, it was eight, and I'm freezing cold, so get down here, right now? Get a taxi or whatever…
B. All right, all right … there's no need to shout!

3
A: Did you have a good weekend?
B: Yeah, the party was great; you were meant to be coming, weren't you?
A: Yeah, I guess I was…
B: So …? We were all waiting for you.
A: Oh, really? I didn't think we'd really made an arrangement … you know, I just didn't feel very well…
B: Oh, really? What's up?
A: Oh, I don't know … I think it's just tiredness, you know…
B: Well, you could've phoned, couldn't you?
A: I left my mobile at work … and … I didn't have your number … your mobile number... that is…
B: Oh, well it was a shame, that's all… we had a great time.
A: Yeah, that's a real shame … you know, I mean I'm dead sorry to have missed it.

2 The thing is, you see, it's just that, you know, I mean, I just

3 I wasn't aware, I didn't mean to, I didn't do it on purpose, I didn't realise

4 I'm terribly sorry / sorry about that! / that's a real shame / I'm dead sorry

5 Student's own answers.

How to...

A

1 1c 2b 3e 4a 5d

2 1 up with 2 off 3 on 4 through 5 forward

3 1 up / on / off / by / over
2 after / for / over / through
3 up / at / over / out
4 off / up / over / out

B

1 Group 1 – c, Group 2 – a, Group 3 – b

2 1 depending 3 rely 4 put 5 switching 8 dragged 9 stayed

3 down – move to a lower position, in – enter / arrive,
off – remove, out – leave, up – move to a higher position

4 1 up 2 out 3 off 4 in 5 down

C

1 somebody's relationship

3 1 broke down 2 have split up 3 fell out 4 cheating on
5 got on with 6 coming on to 7 got off with
8 am falling for

4 (Sample answers)
dress up, dress down, take off, put on, pull up, pull down

Unit 5 | Clubs

Language focus

Overview of passive forms

1 1 It is important for the environment to be protected for the benefit of future generations.
2 As life expectancy increases people should be made to retire at a later age.
3 Too much government money is being spent on defence rather than on health and education.
4 People wouldn't mind being forced to pay higher taxes if they knew the money would be used sensibly.
5 Despite being warned about the need to look after ourselves we still don't do enough exercise.
6 Although many celebrities enjoy being recognised they still have the right to a private life.
7 Children who are brought up in a bilingual household will find it easier to learn other languages in the future.
8 Allowing alcohol to be sold 24 hours a day will inevitably lead to an increase in violent crime.

2 1 was built 2 causes 3 will be holding 4 have been cancelled 5 will be moved 6 was declared 7 noticed
8 were kept

3 Text 1 1 has been jailed 2 being found 3 was seen
4 were called 5 being fired
Text 2 6 were taken 7 being offered 8 was made
9 was led 10 has not been named

Distancing devices

1 two months in jail; former car mechanic

 5.1

Former policeman, Jack McGarvey, was today sentenced to spend the next two years in jail after being found guilty of discharging a firearm in public. It would seem that local residents were woken up by a series of loud bangs, which it is now known were gunshots, at approximately 6am on March the 17th. A passing police patrol car was alerted by the shots and officers arrived at the scene to discover a motorcycle lying in the road with what appeared to be bullet holes in the engine. The owner of the motorcycle, 46-year-old McGarvey, was promptly arrested inside his house, where it appears that he lived alone.
It has not been revealed whether or not McGarvey was under the influence of alcohol at the time of his arrest, although a man matching his description is reported to have been seen acting threateningly and abusing passers-by in the town's main street late on Monday night, having been refused entry to a number of pubs in the area on account of his drunken state. In the quiet suburban street where the incident occurred there is a general feeling that no one should possess a gun let alone use it in this way.
Gary Pride, Independent Radio News.

2 64- / 46-year-old; was seen by a neighbour / local residents were woken by the shots; dusk / 6am; car / motorcycle; The police were called to the scene / A passing police patrol car was alerted by the shots; fourth gun-related crime in the area / quiet suburban street.

3 a5 b6 c3 d4 e1 f– g2

Quantifiers with & without of

The word of required in all cases apart from: 5 too much
6 more and more 9 two 10 none

Vocabulary

Collective nouns for people

1 1 club 2 mob 3 set 4 crowd 5 crew 6 public 7 clique
8 audience 9 gang 10 outfit 11 staff 12 tribes

2 1 mob 2 gang 3 clique

3 audience, club, gang, public, (of) staff, crew

4 set

Collective nouns for things

1 series 2 pile / heap 3 barrage 4 stack 5 bunch, box

Collocations with party

1 party-pooper 2 party 3 party piece 4 throw a party
5 party animal

Verbs & nouns

1 **Nouns only:** techno, scene, rhythm, disco, noise, soul,
leisure
Nouns & Verbs: bar, rave, beat, style, crowd, groove,
sound, DJ

2 1 deejayed 2 raving 3 styled 4 barred 5 beat 6 crowded
7 groove 8 sounds

Listening

1 1g 2a 3f 4c 5d 6h 7e 8b

2a 1 Celtic 2 Boca Juniors 3 Flamengo 4 Barcelona

 5.2

1: Religious differences are the origin of the bitter,
occasionally violent, rivalry between these two Glasgow-
based clubs, known in Scotland as the Old Firm. Rangers
are considered a Protestant and unionist club while Celtic,
a Catholic one. Celtic was set up to raise charitable aid for
the city's Irish immigrants, who were Catholics. Rangers,
on the other hand, was set up by a group of Protestant
men, although unlike Celtic, religion wasn't at the heart of
the club's identity. The rivalry between the clubs dates back
to 1888, when Celtic first beat Rangers 5–2. The Old Firm
derby is one of the most contested matches in the world,
with over 400 games having been played. It is by far the
fiercest football rivalry in Britain.

2: Known to fans in Argentina as Il Manifesto, the rivalry
here is socio-economic in nature. Boca Juniors are the
working-class People's Team, whereas the well-off River
Plate supporters are nicknamed Los Millonarios. Both clubs
were formed in Boca, a poor neighbourhood in the south
of Buenos Aires, home to the city's Italian immigrants. But
in 1938 River Plate moved to a wealthier part of the city.
Known worldwide for the passion of the fans, matches take
place against a background of passionate supporters'
songs, often based on popular Argentine rock band tunes,
with fireworks and flags filling the stadiums. There are also
infrequent violent fights between the most fervent
supporters of both sides. The history of matches between
the two teams shows a slight advantage to Boca Juniors.

3: Known to Brazilians as O Fla-Flu, the rivalry here is a
family affair. Flamengo was founded as an aquatic sports
club while Fluminense was founded as a football club.
Because of that, some members of Flamengo were
originally members of Fluminense as well. In 1911, before
the final match of the Rio de Janeiro Championship, some
Fluminense players argued with the board about the
money they would receive if they won the championship.

Unable to agree ten players left Fluminense and created a
football team in Flamengo. Ironically, perhaps, Flamengo
has grown into the bigger of the two teams, and is now
Rio de Janeiro's most popular club – and some would say
Brazil's favourite team. The atmosphere at the 120,000-
capacity Maracaná Stadium makes a match between these
teams one of the world's great sporting events.

4: The match between Catalan giants FC Barcelona and the
capital's Real Madrid is one of Europe's most spectacular
clashes. Often considered more important than the games
played by the national team, this is not technically a derby
– a match between two rivals in the same city – unlike
those mentioned above. The rivalry here dates back to the
loss of regional autonomy and cultural repression that
Catalonia was subjected to under the Franco dictatorship.
Animosity between the two clubs rose further in 2000 when
Barcelona's star player, Luis Figo, joined the team's arch-
rivals in a £37 million deal. In his first match for Real
Madrid, Barcelona fans reacted furiously, showering Figo
with bottles, lighters and a pig's head.

2b Celtic and Rangers – Glasgow, Scotland

River Plate and Boca Juniors – Buenos Aires, Argentina

Flamengo and Fluminense – Brazil, Rio de Janeiro

Real Madrid and Barcelona – Spain

2c Madrid / Barcelona is the odd one out, because the rivalry
is not between two clubs within the same city, but two
different cities.

3 1 religious 2 greatest / fiercest 3 sing 4 violence / rioting
5 dispute / argument 6 most popular / famous club
7 the national (Spanish) team 8 reception

Zoom In

1 a) hit b) won a match

2 1 do better 2 mix 3 move regularly 4 attacked
5 finished before 6 arrive before

3 1 beat the system 2 beat it 3 you can't beat it
4 beating about the bush 5 It beats me

Guided writing

1 a2 b8 c3 d6 e1 f4

2 1e 2a 3h 4i 5d 6c 7j 8f 9b 10g

3 1 DO 2 DO 3 DON'T 4 DON'T 5 DO 6 DO 7 DON'T 8 DO

4 **5.3**

There are three stages to taking and writing up minutes
effectively. Firstly, before the meeting, look through the
agenda to get an idea of the shape the meeting is expected
to take, and make sure you know who will be taking part –
the names of any committee members, for example.
Stage two is the meeting itself. Just before the meeting gets
underway, pass round a sheet of paper for people to sign to
confirm that they attended. Remember to add the names of
latecomers and ask them to sign the attendance sheet at the
end of the meeting. Meetings being meetings, the order of
proceedings may end up being different from the agenda.
If this is the case, make a clear note of the actual order and
remember to cross-reference this with the agenda when
you write up the minutes later on. Your notes should be
clear and concise and ideally in the form of a list of points;

you may need to use abbreviations, or even shorthand. Do not try to transcribe every word which is said, even if it appears to be a particularly important point. If you do, you will inevitably miss other important information. When you note down individual contributions, write the initials of the contributor next to your notes. If a vote is taken – during elections for committee posts, for example – it is important to specify how the vote was managed, by a show of hands, by calling out, or by a secret ballot. In small meetings it may not be necessary to record who approved, opposed or abstained, but it is vital to record the result: who is elected to which post, or whether a motion is approved or rejected. In the latter case a particular course of action may be approved, in which case a clear note should be made of who is responsible for carrying it out, and what timescale is involved – there may be an agreed deadline, for instance. Then, when the meeting is concluded, note down the time at which it was formally brought to an end.

Stage three is when your notes are written up into their final form. This should be done soon after the meeting so that the proceedings remain as fresh as possible in your memory. Minutes should be typed, in bullet point form, with the name of the organisation, the attendees, date and venue, and the start time at the top. Use formal, non-colloquial language, and avoid adding any comments or opinions of your own, unless they were points which you raised during the meeting. At the end, after discussion of any other business, record the agreed date, time and venue of the next meeting, again if relevant, and record the time at which the meeting was formally drawn to a close. Only after checking your minutes should you submit them to the chair for approval. If approved, the minutes should then be distributed to all those who attended the meeting. They will normally be referred to again, and revised if necessary, at the start of the next meeting.

5 DOs: read the agenda beforehand; familiarise yourself with who is due to take part; ask latecomers to sign the attendance sheet at the end of the meeting; cross-reference the actual order of events with the order on the agenda; make notes as a list, with spaces between lines; use intelligible shorthand or abbreviations; distinguish between people with the same initials; write down motions and the names of the people who propose them; record how people voted; note down the agreed timescale for agreed action; type the minutes, in bullet-point form; use formal language when typing minutes; record the agreed date and venue of the next meeting.

DON'Ts: record or video the meeting (unless you're worried about missing important details); make a note of who seconds a motion (unless it is considered necessary); use colloquial language.

6 1 Treasurer's report 2 It has made money because of an increase in members and fees. 3 Fees will remain the same.

7 Use more formal language, give full names of participants, don't give personal opinions, don't provide irrelevant or trivial information, write minutes in bullet point format.

8 1 Tony Davis, Philippa Harrison
2 Tony: the success of the barbecue and Quiz night – more are planned, disco in spring, tickets for the New Year's Eve dinner are now on sale.
Philippa: organise charity events to raise money for local causes.
3 To look into the possibility of organising fund-raising work. Philippa will draw up a list of charities and fund-raising ideas before the next committee meeting.
4 The committee members are all in favour of the proposal.

A: Moving on to the financial proposals for the forthcoming year. The success of the barbecue and the Quiz night means that similar events are planned for next year. In addition, the committee has decided to hold a second disco in the spring. More details will be available shortly. Lastly, final arrangements have now been made for the New Year's Eve dinner, and tickets will be on sale from Monday. Many members have already reserved tickets, but if anyone else would like to do so this evening, please see me at the end of the meeting.

I would now like to take the opportunity to see if anyone has any further suggestions for fund-raising activities. Please feel free to put forward any ideas you have. Yes, Philippa ... Harrison, isn't it?

B: Yes, thank you. I was wondering if, as the club now appears to be financially secure for the time being, any consideration has been given to the possibility of organising charity events.

A: Such as?

B: Well, raffles, prize draws, that kind of thing? There are plenty of good local causes which the club might be able to help out with.

A: It's not something which we've thought about before, no, but there's no reason why we couldn't do something along those lines, if people thought it might be worthwhile. It would need a fair amount of organising, though, which is something we'd have to take into account.

B: I'd be happy to look into it myself if you like. I've done a little fund-raising work in the past and would love to get back into it.

A: I don't see why not. Would you like to draw up a list of possible charities we could help and come up with some ideas for ways to generate money? Perhaps by the time of the next committee meeting in January?

B: I'd be delighted.

A: OK, thank you. So, Philippa has offered to look into options for charity donations before the next committee meeting. Shall we have a quick show of hands to see if people are happy with that? Those in favour? ...Those against? ...OK, that's unanimous then. Philippa Harrison will...

9 Student's own answer.

Reading

1 1d 2c 3b 4e 5a

2 1T 2F 3F 4F 5T 6T

3 1 don't have to 2 needn't 3 can't 4 need

4 1 is said 2 to be made 3 being stopped 4 have been chosen
5 be paid 6 being made

Listening

1 a2 b6 c7 d4 e5 f1 g3

 (TY.1)

A: I'm joined today by Mike Kipping from Harmonise Consulting who have recently published a report into bullying in the workplace. Mike, welcome to the show.
B: Thanks for inviting me.
A: Bullying, er, is usually associated with kids, but you're saying it occurs between adults as well?
B: Yes, absolutely. We all expect bullying to go on between children, but bullying between adults is a more complicated issue because it is often much less visible and much more subtle. However, there's no doubt that workplace bullying is a very serious problem. Our research shows that almost 25 per cent of employees in the UK claim to have been bullied at work during the last 12 months.
A: Well, they are alarming statistics. Presumably, then, there are a lot of unhappy people at work around the country?
B: Yes, but in fact the consequences go a long way beyond 'unhappiness'. Many victims of bullying go on to suffer chronic mental illness, like depression or eating disorders, and often require extended periods off work. This is also extremely expensive for companies themselves, and ultimately for the economy as a whole.
A: And what kind of jobs are we talking about? Is bullying more of a problem in certain employment sectors than in others?
B: I'm sure it goes on in all sectors. However, it does appear to be more prevalent in those sectors where people are under more pressure and have high degrees of stress.
A: Yes, indeed. And within each sector is seniority a factor?
B: There is a pattern whereby bullying is largely a 'top-down' phenomenon, yes. That is, junior workers might be victimised by their line managers, who in turn might suffer bullying from more senior managers, and so on. But it's not unknown for employees to be bullied by junior colleagues, often as a group. Group bullying, or 'mobbing' is one of the most aggressive forms of workplace bullying.
A: Yes, it sounds very unpleasant. Er … you mentioned reasons for bullying there. What, in fact, are the main causes of workplace bullying?
B: Well, people under stress are more likely to take their frustrations out on their colleagues. But bullying is also rife in competitive work environments in which employees are in some way competing against their colleagues, for clients, say, or for promotion. Other causes might include jealousy, personal rivalry, boredom, distrust…

A: Earlier on you mentioned that workplace bullying is often quite subtle. What did you mean by that?
B: What I mean is that it may not be obvious to people that one of their colleagues is being bullied. Bullying might start out as a casual comment about how someone is dressed, but such comments can escalate into innuendo, which can easily be perceived as sexual harassment. Racial harassment, ageist attitudes, even careless use of bad language can all be interpreted as forms of bullying if they cause psychological distress.
A: So what advice would you have for people who feel they are being bullied at work?
B: With all forms of psychological distress, the golden rule is not to suffer in silence. Remember that the fact that you are being bullied does not mean you are not good at your job – the opposite is more likely to be true – so there is no reason for people to be unsympathetic. Whoever you speak to will want clear evidence that bullying is taking place, though, so get into the habit of writing a diary, however painful or upsetting you might find this. If it really is too painful ask a friend to keep a diary on your behalf.
A: Mike Kipping, thank you very much.

2 1F 2T 3T 4F 5T 6F 7T 8F

3 1 What is clear is that bullying in the workplace is now a very serious problem.
2 By keeping a written record of your experiences as a victim of bullying you will make it easier for people outside the company to help you.
3 Although bullying occurs in all employment sectors, it does appear to be more common in those sectors where people are under more pressure.
4 The fact is, it is not always obvious when bullying is taking place in work environments.
5 There is no reason at all to think that if you are being bullied it is because you are not doing your job well.

Writing

Student's own answer.

Unit 6 Children

Language Focus

Present & past habits

1 1c 2a 3e 4b 5d

2 1 were / used to be 2 spend / will spend 3 will discourage / discourage 4 always / forever 5 would / used to 6 don't / won't 7 are always going on / will go on 8 didn't use to have / didn't have 9 are forever having / have 10 would waste / used to waste

3 to ask her friend Judy for advice about her daughter

4 1 used 2 to 3 always 4 being 5 she 6 would 7 used 8 to 9 is 10 always 11 to 12 be 13 we 14 were 15 didn't 16 use 17 she 18 is 19 will 20 stay

Spoken narrative techniques

2 1 well 2 anyway 3 anyway 4 so 5 anyway 6 so

Well, I must have been about five or six, because my sister is three years younger than me and she was still a baby at the time. Anyway, my dad used to be a teacher and every summer he used to go away for a week on these camping holidays with his school. When my sister and I were a bit older we used to go, with my mum as well, and it became this annual family holiday, but at that time we were both too young so we stayed behind with my mum.

Anyway, although I was only very young I obviously had an artistic streak in me. My dad always kept these old pots of paints and old paintbrushes in the garage, and any chance I got – when my mum and dad weren't looking, obviously – I would sneak in there, help myself to some brushes and some paint, and I would think, 'Right, what can I paint today?' I'd already got in trouble for painting the back door of the house, and the garden path as well if I remember rightly! It was always, well, let's call it an abstract style which was unique to me – lots of different colours, all splattered on pretty much at random.

So, this particular day my dad was away on one of these camping trips, and my mum was having all sorts of trouble with my baby sister, who cried more or less constantly until she was about four. She said something like, 'Go and play outside for a while so Mummy can look after your sister', so I immediately saw this as an opportunity for a bit of artistic expression! I had this friend who lived along the road, about the same age as me, and we were always getting up to mischief – partners in crime, you might say.

Anyway, I must have thought my latest art project was going to be too much for me on my own because I went and knocked on his door and managed to convince him to come out and play with me. Next thing, there we were snooping around in my dad's garage, digging around in all this DIY stuff.

So having already painted the door and the path I needed a new challenge, so we looked around and wondered what we could paint next. Then it struck us! Right in front of our eyes, gleaming in the sunshine on the driveway in front of the house, was…

3 1f 2g 3c 4h 5e 6a 7d 8b

7 1e 2g 3a 4d 5f 6h 7c

Vocabulary

Word-building: Adjectives

1 competitive 2 flirtatious 3 confident 4 sensible
5 rebellious 6 independent 7 manipulative 8 light-hearted

Personality phrases

1 1 the show 2 overindulged 3 loner 4 co-operative 5 laugh
6 fussy 7 sulky 8 control

2 6.3

1 A: She's really bossy, isn't she?
   B: Yeah, she certainly loves running the show, that's for sure.
2 A: He's the typical youngest son, so spoilt!
   B: I know, they are usually really overindulged, aren't they?
3 A: She doesn't mind being on her own, does she?
   B: No, deep down she's a real loner.
4 A: He seems to get on with his parents, doesn't he?
   B: Oh yeah, he's very co-operative; he even helps his mum in the kitchen!
5 A: I think he's so funny.
   B: Absolutely, he's a real laugh at parties.
6 A: She really worries about little things all the time.
   B: I know, it's infuriating, she's so fussy.
7 A: He seems depressed. He won't talk to me.
   B: I know, my son's the same; he's just so sulky sometimes.
8 A: He gets these tantrums; I don't know what to do about it.
   B: I know. It's like he gets out of control, and then it just passes.

3 **Negative:** sulky, run the show, overindulged, fussy, out of control
Positive: co-operative, a laugh
Neutral: a loner

Politically correct language

a) blind b) deaf c) disabled d) chairman e) policeman
f) air hostess g) unemployed h) Black (American)
i) Red Indian j) Eskimo k) wife / husband l) sex
m) Miss/Mrs Smith

Vocabulary Extension

Sexist language

1 1c 2f 3a 4d 5b 6e

2 (Sample answer) The word *woman* could replace *man* in most of the idioms. The effect would be comic or ironic. It is becoming common to hear idioms 1 and 6 used with the word *woman*.

3 1 mankind – humankind 2 man-made – synthetic
3 headmaster – head teacher 4 barmaids – bar staff
5 a man – a plumber 6 chairman – chair / chairperson

Takeaway English

1 1 problems in class / educational difficulties, remedial classes
2 not socialise easily, to talk / make friends 3 listening attentively / without questioning, be independent

2 1 stupid / slow / thick 2 shy / unsociable / timid
3 dependent / clingy

3 Student's own answers.

4 a) slightly out of control b) as good as gold c) she's not clear
d) keeps changing her mind e) gets her own way / what she wants f) won't take 'no' for an answer

1 A: He can get slightly out of control, can't he? Well, I mean when he's with his brother and sister it's worse…

B: Oh yes, when he's at school, he's like, how can I put it? A different person.

A: Yes, he's as good as gold at school.

2 A: She just won't tell me what the problem is … you know she's not … what's the word? Clear, she keeps changing her mind, all the time … it makes me mad.

B: Oh, it must be terrible, yeah.

3 A: I don't know what to do about her, it's just … she's just … you know, she's just got used to getting what she wants. It's like … she really gets her own way.

B: And, it's not as if she wants any old thing, it has to be something expensive, and she really insists, as well you know, she won't take 'no' for an answer.

5 It usually reduces the effect of the adjective or, in some cases, implies the opposite.

6&7 1 food / a little bit hot 2 weather / could be better 3 staff / not the quietest of people 4 a broken glass / it wasn't that expensive 5 (football) match / not exactly a bad result 6 (winning) a holiday / could be worse

6.5

1 Ah … have you eaten a chilli? Listen you might find them a little bit hot…

2 Oh yes, the weather could be better … couldn't it?

3 No, well, the staff are not the quietest of people, no.

4 Oh dear, another glass gone, never mind, it wasn't that expensive, really.

5 It's not exactly a bad result, is it? 5–0.

6 A: I've won, I've won!

B: So you've won a free holiday to the Caribbean? Could be worse, couldn't it?

8 Student's own answers.

How to

1 1b 2e 3f 4c 5d 6a

2 1b 2b 3a 4b 5a 6b 7a 8b

3 a4 b1 c7 d3 e2 f8 g5 h6

4 1 The school currently has students from Libya, Egypt, Kuwait, Saudi Arabia and Iran.

2 People with amputations / amputated limbs sometimes feel uncomfortable in public.

3 Spring can be an uncomfortable time for people with asthma.

4 She has been partially sighted since she was born.

5 Our new MP is a retired judge.

6 The most important quality in a secretary is good organisation.

7 My cousins are very ambitious.

8 Dear Editor,

Unit 7 | Happiness

Language focus

Regrets

1 1a 2d 3e 4c 5f 6b

2 1 We wish we had bought a house five years ago when we had enough money in the bank.

2 She regrets not learning (or not having learned) to drive when she was younger.

3 If his car hadn't broken down on the way to the station he wouldn't have arrived late for the interview.

4 They should have left earlier in the afternoon to avoid the rush hour.

5 I would have loved to be able (or would love to have been able) to go to her wedding.

6 Had the alleged victim told the truth the defendant would never (or never would) have been convicted.

3 1 I wish I **had** studied a bit harder when I was at school.

2 I regret **having** too much to drink last night!

3 I'm so sleepy. I shouldn't **have had** such a big lunch.

4 I would like **to** have started studying English at an earlier age.

5 **Had** I done more exercise in the past I would be fitter now.

The past with present or future meaning

1 1e 2a 3f 4b 5d 6c

2 (Sample answers)

1 I wish I had a girlfriend.

2 It's time someone emptied that bin.

3 If you weren't with me I'd get a tattoo.

4 Supposing we ordered a pizza instead?

5 Wouldn't you rather we saw this one?

6 I'd sooner we went a bit further over there.

3 Student's own answers.

Vocabulary

Emotional ups and down

1 a) positive b) negative c) negative d) negative e) positive f) negative

2 1 cheers 2 made 3 finished 4 freaked 5 gets 6 makes

Vocabulary extension

Mood swings

1 **Positive:** to be on an up, to be fired-up, to be over the moon

Negative: to be on a downer, to be the last straw, to be gloomy, to be on edge

2 a to be the last straw b to be overwhelmed

3 1 on an up 2 the last straw 3 on edge 4 overwhelmed 5 on a downer 6 gloomy 7 fired-up 8 over the moon

Humour

1 1 grin. Grin means to smile, but the others are ways of laughing. All words can act as verbs or nouns.

2 fun. Fun is used for talking about something that is enjoyable. The other adjectives are used for talking about something or someone that makes you laugh.

3 tease. The others are types of jokes or plays on words.

4 sarcastic. The others are types of humour; 'sarcastic' is an adjective which describes a type of humour;

5 laughter. The others are people, although 'comic' can also be used as an adjective

6 snigger. The others mean to 'laugh at somebody'; 'snigger' means to laugh in an unkind way.

2 1 funny 2 grin 3 teased / mocked 4 giggling / chuckling 5 laugh (noun) 6 comic 7 fun 8 puns

Reading

Advertising techniques

1 1c 2e 3d 4a 5g 6b 7h 8f

2 (Sample answers)
1 marks: signals
2 cachet: prestige, a special quality that makes people admire someone or something
3 enhanced: improved (by making something more attractive or valuable)
4 seal of approval: something that you say that shows you admire someone or something
5 catchy: a tune or phrase that attracts your attention and is easy to remember
6 vignette: a short but interesting piece of writing or section of a film
7 flawed: wrong; spoiled by something such as a fault
8 state-of-the-art: using the latest technology and most advanced ideas and features

3 **Product:** 1 an iron 2 a car 3 a watch
4 shampoo / conditioner 5 an airline company
Consumer: 1 a housewife 2 a 30+ person 3 professional man 4 women 5 ordinary people

🎧 7.1

1 Don't let your family leave the house with creased shirts! The new Smoothline professional iron has a powerful shot of steam for those stubborn creases and its stainless steel plate is resistant to any scratches. Smoothline iron now comes with an integrated cartridge for extended life. Time to feel proud of your family! Smoothline – professional ironing at its best.
2 You wanted to study sociology, but your father told you that economics was a better option professionally. You didn't like your job but your friends told you that you wouldn't find anything better. You never wanted to get married but your family insisted and now … do you live for yourself or for others? With the Sorensso Scirocco you regain control. Sirensso – you are the driver.
3 Don't give in to pressure. The Mountain Hours series. A genuine leather strap with folding buckle. Steel casing. Sapphire crystal. Double protection crown. Water resistant to 200 metres. It says more about you than your bank balance *ever* can. True Time. Made in Switzerland since 1860.
4 'Dull, thin hair?' asks Dr Andrew Jay from Confidence laboratories, Paris. Watch the transformation with Max Hair from Hair Health. A brand new, scientifically tested three-step system to give your hair the body you've always wanted. The body-boost shampoo, weightless conditioner and a revolutionary roots lifter combine to increase the thickness of your hair. The result: you're bigger in the one place you want to be. Confidence – a uniquely boosting experience.
5 You know, the moment I got off the plane, I could feel the difference and I saw the blue sky, the endless sunshine, the friendly faces welcoming us and I thought … this is the life! And all this waiting for you just three hours away with Quickfly. It's a place that you makes you feel good in no time at all. I loved it and I would definitely go back again. Fly to Greece with Quickfly – luxury travelling at budget prices! What a land! What a life! Paradise is just around the corner.

4 1 guilt, blinded by science 2 association of ideas, key words
3 association of ideas 4 before and after, ask the expert
5 slice of life, association of ideas

Zoom In

1 good and bad times / uneven

2 1 up to my ears 2 time is up 3 up to something 4 up to you
5 wrong way up 6 on the up and up 7 ups and downs
8 up-and-coming

3 1b 2c 3a 4b 5d 6d 7a 8c

Guided writing

1 A Quality Assurance Trainer

2 1A 2E 3C 4G 5F 6B 7D 8H

3 Do not list all your initial qualifications from school; Do not include references in the CV; Do not try to use a wide range of elaborate fonts

4 Tip 1 – Nationality, Tip 2 – Employment History,
Tip 3 – Not illustrated (Employment History)
Tip 4 – Education Tip 5 – Interests Tip 6 – References
Tip 7 – Employment History
Tip 8 – Not illustrated (CV is in one font)
Tip 9 – Career Objective Tip 10 – Personal Profile

5&6 Student's own answers.

Unit 8 | Numbers

Language focus

Modals in the past

1 1 Eric Myler 2 Doreen Wallace; Micky Trotter; Maggie Myler
3 Doreen Wallace: she couldn't afford to pay the rent if Myler increased it, as he had threatened to do. Micky Trotter: he hated Myler; Myler was having an affair with Micky's ex-wife; he thought Myler was mean because he was going to increase the rent. Maggie Myler: she knew her husband was having an affair; she wanted to get his life insurance money.

2 1 can't have killed 2 might have wanted 3 would have been damaged 4 may have had 5 would have increased
6 could have pushed 7 wouldn't have been 8 must have changed 9 could have fallen 10 ought to have realised

3 Student's own answers.

4 Doreen Wallace killed Eric Myler by pushing him out of her window, while he was changing her light bulb.

🎧 8.1

Well, I soon realised that suicide was out of the question. Quite simply, Eric Myler can't have killed himself by jumping off the roof because the door to the roof was still locked, so my suspicions turned to the wife. I considered the possibility that Maggie Myler might have wanted to kill her husband because she was jealous of his affairs. That would be a motive, but what about the method? The only obvious option for her would be to push him out of the window of their flat, but having visited the flat, I realised Mrs Myler can't have pushed her husband out of the window because her window box would've been damaged which it clearly wasn't.
Mickey Trotter may have had a motive too, because Myler was having an affair with his ex-wife. Not only that, he also admitted hating the way Myler treated his tenants and explained that if Myler hadn't died, he would've increased the rent the following month. So, two motives in fact. If his window hadn't been nailed shut, Mickey Trotter could've pushed Myler out of it, but, as it happened, there was no way Trotter could've done it, so my attention switched to my only other suspect.
Clearly, Doreen Wallace wouldn't have been able to afford the rent if Myler had doubled it, so she had a clear motive for killing

him, but how would an old lady manage to kill a man like Myler? Well, remember the light bulb which she said she'd changed? Given her age and frail physical state, it was clear to me that Mrs Wallace wouldn't have been able to change the light bulb on her own, so someone else must've changed it for her: her landlord, for instance. Myler could have fallen out of Mrs Wallace's window while he was changing the light bulb, but why would Mrs Wallace have lied about the light bulb and about seeing Myler fall past her window?

The answer lies in Mrs Wallace's statement. Remember how she said she'd called the police before going down to the street? Mrs Wallace ought to have realised that anyone with their eyes open would've noticed she didn't have a phone. Three lies from the same suspect? Case closed, I'm afraid. Doreen Wallace called Eric Myler to her flat to change a light bulb, then, while he was still at the top of the ladder, she simply pushed him out of her open window, all in a desperate attempt to stop her rent increasing. Well, Mrs Wallace won't have to worry about the rent where she's going.

5 1a 2c 3b 4c

6

1

A: Look at all this mud on the carpet!

B: Oh! It wasn't me! Ally was playing football outside, so if you ask me he must have done it.

2

A: So who do you think took the money? Do you think it might have been Denise?

B: Well, I suppose she could have done it but I just don't think she would do that.

3

A: Has John finished that report yet?

B: Er, I'm not absolutely sure, but he should have done it because he's been writing it all morning.

4

A: Don't say a word! I know what you're thinking! It's terrible. And it cost me nearly £50!

B: Well, I must say you do look a bit weird. Didn't you know

Nicky could have done it for you? She always does my hair.

Discourse markers

1 1b 2a

2 1b 2c 3c 4a 5a 6c

Vocabulary

Expressions with numbers

1 1f 2a 3e 4b 5c 6d

2 1 it's back to square one 2 to have a one track mind 3 it takes two to tango 4 it's first come, first served 5 to be in seventh heaven 6 it's six of one and half a dozen of the other

3 1 it's back to square one 2 it takes two to tango 3 have a one track mind 4 it's six of one and half a dozen of the other 5 first come, first served 6 was in seventh heaven

4 1 I thought I had made up my mind to take the job, but now I'm having second thoughts.

2 As always, I was rushing and I handed in the work at the eleventh hour.

3 Since I got back from the health farm, I feel like a million dollars.

4 I didn't really have a proper sleep, just forty winks.

5 I wouldn't trust him, he's says one thing and then does another. He's so two-faced.

6 It's incredible! Since I won first prize, I've just been on cloud nine.

Number prefixes

a) duplicate b) decade c) centipede d) multitude e) monorail f) polyglot g) binoculars h) solitaire i) unisex j) kilobyte k) millisecond l) quartet

Listening & Vocabulary

1 1 £2.60

2 19, 10, 2

3 doubles, 6–2 / 6–3, five, 30–40, first

4 fourth, 250 m, a quarter of a billion, fifth, 63

5 12, 15, 33, 44, 49, 50, 37, 2.8 million dollars

6 01552 733300, 01552 777922, 9 a.m., 8.30 p.m., 01552 386446, 2873-5266-37/1

1

A: Anything else, sir?

B: Er, yeah, can I have a double espresso?

A: Double espresso comin' up, anything else?

B: No, thanks … er, to take away, sorry…

A: That's two pound sixty please.

2

Clear skies will bring a drop in temperature over much of the country. This afternoon there will be a high of 19 degrees in the South East, but temperatures will be lower elsewhere, with highs of only 10 degrees in many northern areas. Temperatures will drop to 2 degrees overnight, with frost in some areas.

3

A: So, let's go over to Centre Court and Kevin Sanders…

B: Hello, well it's a full house here in Centre Court to watch this men's doubles final … the Spaniards starting the stronger 6–2 and 6–3 but it's gone to five sets as you can see, and it's 30–40 to the Americans in this first game of the…

4

A: That's right, the majority of people think that but look carefully at the statistics … and you'll see that the fourth biggest country in the world is actually Indonesia, there are nearly 250 million people living there, almost a quarter of a billion, only just behind the United States in fact, and way ahead of Brazil, which is the fifth most populated country in the world. Now, let's move on to population density, turn to page 63…

5

A: Just before our Friday film, a reminder of tonight's lotto results. The winning combination was 12, 15, 33, 44, 49 and 50. The Bonus Ball was 37. It looks as if there's one winner who will take home an estimated jackpot of 2.8 million dollars.

6

Welcome to Powerline Power Supplies Limited. To report a fault or leak, please dial our Emergency Line on 01552 733300. To register Powerline as your power supplier, please contact our Connections Team on 01552 777922 between 9.00am and 8.30pm Monday to Friday. For complaints, dial 01552 386446, quoting reference number 2873-5266-37/1.

2 1 A coffee bar. He's ordering an espresso coffee.

2 On TV or radio. It's a weather forecast.

3 On TV or radio. It's a live broadcast of a tennis match.

4 The classroom. The teacher is talking about population of different countries.

5 TV. The presenter is announcing the lotto results.

6 A recorded message on the Powerline telephone.

3 1 football 2 tennis 3 golf 4 ice skating / diving 5 swimming 6 basketball

Vocabulary & Reading

1 a) mathematical b) publications c) popularity d) offerings
e) abbreviation f) daily g) ability h) addition i) numerical
j) required k) challenging l) addictive m) simplicity
n) improvement o) increasing p) satisfaction

2 a) immense b) catchier c) boom d) arithmetic e) grid
f) craze g) brainpower h) tabloid

3 (Sample answers)
1 Some people call Kakuro 'Cross Sums'.
2 The name Kakuro comes from Japan.
3 One of the reasons for the game's popularity is that the rules are simple.
4 People don't get tired of playing Kakuro because it is so flexible.
5 Unlike the Rubik's Cube craze Kakuro is not a sort of status symbol.
6 It is clear that Kakuro helps to sell newspapers.

4 Student's own answer.

How to

1 a) thirty-seven
b) seven hundred and fifty-two
c) five thousand, six hundred and ninety-two
d) seventy-eight thousand and sixteen
e) eight hundred and sixty-four thousand, two hundred and ninety
f) seven million, one hundred and four thousand, three hundred and seventy-eight

2 When we say numbers larger than 99 in English, we use
and after the word *hundred*, except when the number is
an exact multiple of 100.
573 **five hundred and seventy-three**
700 **seven hundred**
We also use **and** after the words *thousand, million,* etc. if
the number which follows is less than 100.
4,009 **four thousand and nine**
3,000,042 **three million and forty-two**

Types of numbers

1 1 €43; $0.34; 43p
2 $^3/_4$; $^1/_3$; $^1/_4$
3 4 x 3 = 12; 4 + 3 = 7; 4 − 3 = 1; 4 ÷ 3 = 1.33
4 4.43
5 43%
6 √34
7 4^3
8 3
9 4
10 $^4/_3$
11 4.03pm; 03.40
12 43°

2 1 forty-three euros; thirty-four cents; forty-three pence/p
2 three-quarters; a third; a quarter
3 four times three is / equals twelve; four plus three is /
equals seven; four minus / take-away three is / equals one;
four divided by three is / equals one point three recurring
4 four point four three
5 forty-three per cent
6 the square root of 34
7 four cubed / four to the power of three
8 three
9 four
10 four-thirds
11 four 'o' three pm / three minutes past four; three forty /
'o' three forty hours
12 forty-three degrees

four; four multiplied by three is twelve or four times three
equals twelve; four-thirds; forty-three per cent; forty-three
euros; three; forty-three degrees; four plus three is seven or
four and three equals seven; three-quarters; four minus
three is one or four take away three equals one; the square
root of thirty-four; thirty-four cents; four point four three; a
third; four 'o' three pm or three minutes past four in the
afternoon; forty-three p; a quarter; four divided by three
equals one point three three; three forty or twenty to four;
four cubed or four to the power of three

3 1c 2e 3a 4d 5b

4 1 13.25 2 £3.49 3 84.16 4 3.9% 5 200

5 a) 16.18 b) £2.25 c) 5715.28 d) 200,000 e) 1 $^1/_4$

1: The next train to arrive at platform 7 will be the delayed
13.25 from Exeter St David's, scheduled to arrive at London
Paddington at 15.48. Please note that this train is running
slightly later than scheduled, and is now expected to arrive
at London Paddington at 16.18.

2: Don't miss this week's offers on all frozen foods! Steak
and kidney pies down 50p from £2.99 to £2.49. Family-size
pizzas down from £3.49 to £1.85. And this week's 'Saver
Special' – buy any £1.80 tub of ice-cream and get a second
tub for 25% of the normal price! That's two tubs for only
£2.25!

3: Financial news now and following the release of
yesterday's inflation figures, the markets have opened
strongly on the Stock Exchange this morning, with the
FTSE 100 share index initially jumping 84.16 points to
5722.62 within the first few minutes of trading, although
it has now dropped back slightly to 5715.28.

4: The fact is that this government's policies have brought
about an economic decline of such magnitude that inflation
is now running at 3.9%, compared with a high of only 2.5%
during our last government, and there are already nearly
200,000 more unemployed than when this government
came to power, the total having risen to over 800,000.

5: As you come into the town, go through the lights and
then after three-quarters of a mile, turn left onto Brookvale
Avenue. About 200 metres further on you'll pass a pub on
the right, and, after another 400 metres or so, take the road
off to your left. Keep going for another one and a quarter
miles and you'll see the house on the right, just before the
church.

Unit 9 | Space

Language focus

Giving information about things

1 Student's own answers.

2
a) pseudo-pornographic; specially-designed
b) video cameras; diary room
c) its format; the show's success
d) no media contact; some of their weekly allowance;
e) in a psychiatric hospital; within view of video cameras
f) addictive to watch; eager to make
g) providing; communicated
h) live soap operas; the people with the most nominations
i) whom...; which...

3 1) 3 2) 1 3) 2 4) 2 5) 3 6) 1

 9.1

1: I have to say, I used to think it was utter rubbish – chewing gum for the eyes if you like – but once I watched a couple of shows I was completely hooked. It's hard to explain, but then who cares if no one really understands why it's so popular? The thing is, you assume that the contestants are going to, you know, perform for the cameras, but after a while you realise that they're just being natural, kind of forgetting they're on camera. Like a real-life version of that Jim Carrey film, *The Truman Show*. Absolutely gripping television, even when nothing happens!

2: For me, the most interesting series was the celebrity version which was won by the only contestant who wasn't actually a celebrity, this girl called Chantelle. She had to pretend she was a singer in a group and convince everyone she was genuinely famous, even though the group didn't even exist. As long as none of the others guessed the truth she'd be allowed to stay in the house. And, sure enough, she ended up winning! And then people wonder why the show is so popular! As far as I'm concerned it's blindingly obvious. Watching her win it I thought, well, if that doesn't say it all about the idea of reality TV and the concept of celebrity, I don't know what does.

3: Well, it's a bit of a mystery, if you ask me. You can't deny how much it's captured the public's imagination – the viewing figures prove that – but you really do either love it or hate it. There are friends of mine who are cultured, intelligent people and yet they're addicted to it. They all say, try watching one show and you won't be able to drag yourself away from it. So I did just that, and fell asleep after ten minutes. If I want to see reality happening I'd rather go and sit in the park to see it rather than sit glued to the TV screen hour after hour.

4 1 hard to explain 2 on camera 3 real-life 4 who wasn't actually a celebrity 5 none of the others 6 Watching 7 a bit of a mystery 8 friends of mine 9 TV screen

5 1f 2e 3a 4i 5d 6g 7h 8c 9b

Inversion after negative expressions

1 1 to express concern at plans for the construction of a sports centre, outline objections to it, and ask for support in making an official complaint 2 neighbours

2 1 Not only 2 At no 3 Little does 4 Only 5 no sooner 6 On no occasion 7 should 8 Only then

Vocabulary

Expressions with space

1 stare into space 2 outer space 3 advertising space 4 enclosed space 5 spaced out 6 space of time 7 parking space 8 breathing space 9 a waste of space 10 space-age

Listening

1 1e 2d 3b 4a 5f 6c

 9.2

1
A: Look … you see, it keeps crashing for no apparent reason.
B: Yeah, I think I know what the problem is.
A: What?
B: Well, you don't have enough capacity on your hard drive.
A: Oh, how stupid!
B: You see, all these files that you don't use anymore, they're not leaving you enough space, you're gonna have to erase all of this…

2
A: Just write your full name there.
B: OK.
A: In capital letters, remember, as you would like it to appear on your card.
B: Right… Oh, my name takes up too much space, actually.
A: Well, it doesn't matter if the last few letters are cut off, does it?
B: I don't know, shouldn't it be my full name if it's a credit card?
A: No, don't worry…

3
A: So, what do you make of this one, then?
B: I love its energy; the play of light, the colours, everything, it's so dynamic!
A: Yes, and if you compare it with his early work, you can see a whole different concept of space…
A: Yes, well, he's created a much more three-dimensional space, don't you think?
B: Of course… OK, now, have you seen this one over here, I would say that this was his masterpiece…

4
A: Well, I think you should knock that wall down for a start.
B: But, that's a holding wall, you know, it's going to be complicated…
A: No…
B: …and expensive.
A: Well, maybe, yeah … but think of the space you'll make for yourself, and the sun'll come pouring in here. At the moment you've got half the flat in total darkness … you don't realise it but that wall really gets in the way.

5
A: So, will your child be enrolling in September?
B: Well, we're very interested of course, but it's a question of her marks, really.
A: Of course, I understand. Rest assured we'll find a space for her, if all goes well with the exams.
B: Thank you so much…

6
A: She's gone.
B: I know, and she's not coming back either.
A: So, what are you going to do?
B: I don't know.
A: I mean … you should take up something new, anything, to fill up the space…
B: Yeah, it's very empty without her...

2a 1 space on a hard drive 2 space on a credit card 3 sense of space in a painting 4 space in a house 5 space in a school 6 space left by a person's absence

2b 1 leave enough space 2 takes up too much space 3 create space 4 make space 5 find a space 6 fill up the space

Urban areas

1 1 shanty town 2 gentrified area 3 townships 4 squats 5 ghettos 6 suburbs

2 **Negative connotation:** shanty town, township, squat, ghetto

Zoom In

1 over 465,000 square metres of floor space = use 3 overtake = use 4

2 a3 b6 c1 d5 e8 f2 g7 h4

3 1 overslept 2 overbooked 3 overcook 4 overspend 5 overworked 6 oversimplifying

Vocabulary Extension

People and spaces

a2 b5 c10 d8 e7 f1 g9 h6 i4 j3

Reading

1 (Sample answers) apartment blocks, a shopping mall, a 4000-seat performance hall, hotel rooms

2 1 True 2 True 3 False – Las Vegas remains the biggest, though this may change in the future 4 False – they are the newly wealthy 5 True (legally)

3 1 to house 2 deluxe 3 to fashion 4 venture 5 revenue 6 flood

Guided writing

1 b)

2 Student's own answer.

3 (Sample answers)
a) Proposal for the redevelopment of the harbour area
b) Development plan
c) The aim is to develop the site so as to ensure maximum benefit to the town whilst minimising potential negative consequences for the surrounding area.
d) An adjoining youth club
e) Fitness classes will be offered
f) Current leisure facilities are inadequate
g) A sports centre and youth club will undoubtedly benefit the town and its residents, providing much-needed facilities with minimum associated risk.

4 1 boast 2 state-of-the-art 3 wide range 4 rectify 5 conveniently located 6 cater for 7 suitably-equipped 8 guarantee 9 undoubtedly 10 much-needed

5 Student's own answer.

Unit 10 | The end

Language focus

All / every / each

1 1 all doubt 2– 3 Every great dream 4 every single thing 5 all of the fun 6– 7– 8 each is inevitably disappointed

2 1e 2c 3f 4b 5a 6h 7d 8g

3 1 of each 2 each 3 Every 4 each 5 each of 6 every 7 all 8 each of

Participle clauses

1 1a 2h 3b 4f 5e 6d 7g 8c

2 a) Raised b) Having made c) Regarded d) Earning e) Created f) Having won g) Capturing h) ending

Vocabulary

Euphemisms

1 1 to pass away – to die, 2 our loved ones – the dead, 3 loss – death, 4 to kick the bucket – to die, 5 to put an animal down – to kill, 6 a better place – heaven, 7 grief therapist – undertaker / funeral director, 8 to terminate – to kill, 9 the dearly departed – the dead, 10 clients – corpses / dead bodies.

2 formal: 2, 7, 8, 9, 10 neutral: 1, 3, 5, 6 informal: 4

3 1 asylum seekers – refugees – (c)
2 The big C – Cancer – (a)
3 to powder my nose – go to the toilet – (b)
4 sex workers – prostitutes – (d)
5 the news – something unmentionable – (c)
6 casualties – dead people – (b); intervention – attack – (c)
7 senior citizens – retired people – (d)
8 pro-life – anti-abortion movement / pro-choice – pro-abortion movement – (b)
9 adult movie – pornographic movie – (c)

4a 1b 2f 3g 4e 5d 6h 7a 8c

b 1 military 2 corporate 3 corporate 4 corporate 5 military 6 social 7 social 8 social

5 1 customer service representative 2 neutralised, target 3 jobseekers 4 outsourced 5 freedom fighters 6 taxpayers 7 downsized 8 counter culture

Film language

1h 2f 3c 4g 5e 6a 7d 8b 9j 10i

Film genres

1h 2i 3g 4f 5j 6a 7b 8c 9d 10e

Takeaway English

1 Student's own answers.

2 1

1b 2a 3d 4c

2

1 The man is too arrogant and refuses her an autograph.
2 The woman turns down the man's invitation very rudely.
3 The man mistakenly thinks that the dead person committed suicide; the woman corrects him by saying that it was an accident. 4 The woman insists that the man drink alcohol, forgetting that he was an ex-alcoholic.

3

1 'I don't do autographs, you see.'
2 'Oh, I'm not that desperate, Kenneth!'
3 'So young … to take your own life at that age…'
4 'That's the last time I offer you something decent to drink.'

4

(Sample answers)
1 Of course, I would be delighted.
2 I don't think it's the right thing to do.
3 So young to lose a life. Please accept my condolences / my deepest sympathies.
4 I can appreciate that.

 10.1

1

A: That was wonderful, what a truly wonderful performance!
B: Oh, please, well that's very kind of you.
A: Just wonderful!
B: Well, yes, I wasn't bad, was I?
A: No, you were stunning, stunning, there's no other word to describe it. Could I have your autograph?
B: Oh, now, there's just one thing here … I don't do autographs, you see…

2

A: It's getting late…
B: Yes, it is a bit.
A: I was wondering whether…
B: Yes? What?
A: I was wondering whether you might come back home with me…
B: Oh, I'm not that desperate, Kenneth!

3

A: I was so sorry to hear about your … sad news.
B: Oh, don't worry.
A: I really don't know what to say.
B: It's OK, there's nothing really to say.
A: So young … to take your own life at that age…
B: She didn't take her own life, you fool … it was an accident, didn't they tell you?
A: Sorry, I didn't know.

4

A: C'mon have a drink on us!
B: No, it's really OK, I don't drink.
A: C'mon. We've got some champagne open … are you telling me you're turning down our best champagne?
B: I would really prefer something without alcohol, if that's OK. You see, I ca…
A: I don't believe it! Well, that's the last time I offer you something decent to drink.
B: I don't drink, I never drink; I'm an alcoholic. It's best for me not to touch the stuff…
A: I see … I'm sorry, I didn't remember…

3 1 It'd be a pleasure. 2 What on earth's the matter?
3 in case you hadn't heard. 4 Please accept my condolences.
5 Please be our guest. 6 I can appreciate that.

 10.2

1

A: That was wonderful, what a truly wonderful performance!
B: Oh, please, well that's very kind of you.
A: Just wonderful!
B: Well, you know. I've been doing it for years…
A: No, you were stunning, stunning, there is no other word to describe it. Could I have your autograph?
B: Well, of course madam. It'd be a pleasure.

2

A: It's getting late…
B: Yes, it is a bit
A: I was wondering whether…
B: Kenneth, are you OK? What on earth's the matter?
A: I was wondering whether you might come back home with me…
B: Oh, don't you think we're getting a bit old for that kind of thing?

3

A: I was so sorry to hear about your … sad news
B: Oh, don't worry!
A: I really don't know what to say
B: It's OK, there's nothing really to say.
A: So young … to take your own life at that age…
B: Well, I have to put you right on one thing … it was an accident actually, in case you hadn't heard…
A: Oh, I'm so terribly sorry. Please accept my condolences.

4

A: C'mon have a drink on us!
B: No, it's really OK, I don't drink.
A: C'mon. We've got some champagne open … can I really not offer you a glass? Please be our guest…
B: I would really prefer something without alcohol, if that's OK. You see, I ca…
A: Of course, I understand…
B: I don't drink, I never drink, I'm an alcoholic. It's best for me not to touch the stuff…
A: Yes, I can appreciate that…

4 (Sample answers)
1 on hearing the news of a death
2 when someone gives you a present you weren't expecting
3 when someone offers you more food which you don't want
4 when you can't remember someone's name in a formal situation
5 when you forget an important appointment
6 when you do something wrong and want to apologise

How to

1 Best regards; Best wishes; With love; Yours faithfully

2 a) T b) F c) F d) T e) F

4 1b 2a 3a 4c 5c

5 1 b, e, c, d, a 2 a, e, d, c, b 3 b, d, e, c, a 4 b, d, a, c, e

6 1 two friends, before one of them goes on holiday
2 two friends, after a dinner party
3 a customer booking a table in a restaurant
4 two friends tentatively arranging to go out for a drink

10.3

1

A. Anyway, I won't keep you because you must have loads of things to organise.
B. OK, well, I'll send you a text when we get there – it'll be cheaper than phoning.

A. Right-o. Have a lovely time. And send us a postcard!

B. Will do. Speak to you in a couple of weeks. Ta-ta.

A. Ta-ta.

2

A. Well, I'd better be off, otherwise I'll miss my train.

B. Yes, it's the last one as well.

A. So, thanks again for the meal. You must let me know the recipe.

B. OK, I'll e-mail it to you tomorrow. Look after yourself.

A. Thanks, Jo. Take care.

3

A. So that's a table for four at 9.30 on Saturday.

B. That's right. Oh, and non-smoking if possible.

A. No problem at all. We're actually non-smoking throughout.

B. Oh yes, of course. So, we'll see you on Saturday then.

A. OK. Cheerio then.

4

A. Right, I must dash. I'm late for work. Good to see you, anyway.

B. Yeah, we should arrange to go out sometime for a few beers.

A. Yeah, let's do that. I could do with a night out. I'll give you a ring.

B. Cool. Cheers, then.

A. Cheers mate. Have a good one.

7 1 I won't keep you; I'd best be off; I must dash

2 Have a good one

3 Take care; Look after yourself

4 Speak to you in a couple of weeks; we'll see you on Saturday

5 Ta-ta; Cheerio; Cheers

2 Test yourself!

Reading

1 1f 2a 3c 4e 5b

2 1F 2F 3F 4F 5T

3 1 What's more 2 although 3 Similarly 4 Nevertheless
5 However

4 1 Having become 2 Having worked 3 Being 4 Playing
5 Packed

Listening

1 1b 2c 3a 4e 5d

 TY.2

Daryl

If I'm honest with you, my answer would have to be … nothing. Before you start thinking I must be a really miserable whatchamacallit, what I mean is that I like to think of happiness as being something which comes from inside me, in other words, being happy is a conscious decision I can make whenever I need to, when I'm under pressure, say. Of course, there are times when I have to work harder to, if you like, 'be happy', but however much of a struggle it might be, it's always within my grasp. I had a phase a few years ago when I was really into Buddhism and I learnt how to meditate. And it was meditation that taught me how to control my emotions.

Andres

There's only one thing I can think of which has always made me happy whenever I've been lucky enough to get it, and that's lots and lots of cash! They say money doesn't bring happiness, but that's absolute rubbish if you ask me. It might not make you happy in itself, but it lets you get hold of the things that do, and that's good enough for me! Put it this way, if I offered a hundred people a million pounds, how many would say, 'If it's all the same to you mate, I'd rather not?' I'll tell you how many – none! That says it all, doesn't it?

Julia

An evening in, lying on the sofa with a bottle of red wine and an entire series of *Friends* on DVD. *Friends* is my favourite TV series of all time, and even though I must've seen every episode at least half a dozen times, I never seem to get tired of watching it. Any time I have half an hour to spare I pick a DVD out and watch an episode. It's easy entertainment which doesn't require you to think too hard but at the same time it's an example of a group of actors doing a perfect job with a perfect script. And of course it's very funny as well. In some ways it gets better the more you watch it, but then that may depend on how good the wine is!

Trevor

There was a politician – I think it was Margaret Thatcher – who always said that happiness was a ticked-off list, and I feel a bit like that myself. It's like when I wake up in the morning I have this list of things in my head that I need to do during the day, and then at night I kind of run through the list and tick off the things I've done. The more things I've managed to get done, the happier I feel, with myself and about the day as a whole. And the more unpleasant the things I've done are, the happier I feel about having done them – like I'm rewarding myself with happiness!

Michelle

I've always really enjoyed playing tennis, not to any great standard, but just with friends, you know, to relax and unwind at the weekend. And every now and again – maybe once per match – I somehow manage to play the most amazing shot. Sometimes it's an ace when I'm serving, other times it might be a winner down the line, or a perfectly placed lob. Of course, I never know when it's going to happen, but when it does I get this surge of adrenalin the moment I hit the ball, like a burst of intense happiness. And for a fraction of a second I feel like the best player in the world!

2 1F 2F 3T 4F 5F

3 1 used to 2 are always insisting 3 is forever 4 would
5 will hit

4 1 every time 2 all of them 3 each episode
4 all of the things 5 in each / in each of them

Writing

Student's own answer.